SCHOLASTIC
ATLAS
OF THE
UNITED
STATES

SCHOLASTIC
ATLAS
OF THE
UNITED
STATES

David Rubel

An Agincourt Press Book

SCHOLASTIC
REFERENCE

To Abraham Rosman and Robert Schmeling, on their seventieth
and eightieth years, respectively
            —D. R.

Dedicated with love to our parents
            —Tilman and Sherry

Copy Editor: Ron Boudreau
Proofreader: Laura Matteau

Art Direction and Production: Oxygen Design
Interior Design, Maps, Illustrations: Sherry Williams, Tilman Reitzle
Image Research: Deborah Goodsite, Julia Rubel
Cover design: Peter Koblish, Nancy Sabato

Special thanks are due Marshall Creighton and Dan Henke of the United States Geological
Survey, Bob Sann, Tracie Cayford of the Utah Travel Council, Amy Hastert of the Wisconsin
Department of Tourism, Jay Hammond of the Kentucky Department of Surface Mining, and
Chris Walker of the *Emporia Gazette*.

For photo credits, see p. 144.

Library of Congress Cataloging-in-Publication Data
Rubel, David.
Scholastic atlas of the United States/by David Rubel.
p. cm.—(Scholastic Reference)
Includes index and glossary.
Summary: Maps of each state in the United States, organized by region, accompanied by
facts and figures.
ISBN 0-590-72562-9
1. United States—Maps for children. 2. Children's atlases.   99-26960
[1. United States—Maps. 2. Atlases.] I. Title. II. Series.   CIP
G1200.R8 2000 <G&M>   MAPS
912.73—DC21

10 9 8 7 6 5 4 3 2 1   0/0 01 02 03 04 05

Contents

LEGEND
The legend printed above each map explains the meaning of its symbols, colors, and patterns. The legend also contains a scale, which shows the relationship of map distances to actual distances.

STATE NAME ORIGIN
Above the name of each state is an explanation of that name's origin.

STATE FLAG
Below the name of each state is a picture of that state's flag.

STATE LOCATOR MAP
This map shows the location of each state in relation to other continental states.

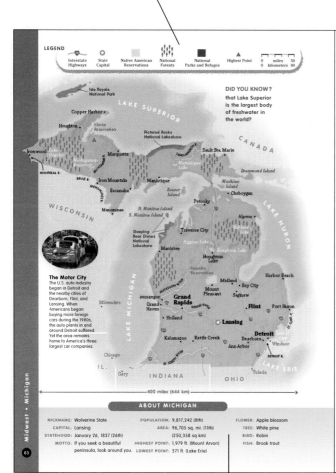

LEGEND

Interstate Highways · State Capital · Native American Reservations · National Forests · National Parks and Refuges · Highest Point · 0 miles 50 · 0 kilometers 80

DID YOU KNOW?
that Lake Superior is the largest body of freshwater in the world?

Isle Royale National Park
LAKE SUPERIOR
Copper Harbor
Houghton · L'Anse Reservation
Ironwood · Pictured Rocks National Lakeshore
Marquette · Sault Ste. Marie
CANADA
Iron Mountain · Drummond Island
Escanaba · Manistique · Mackinac Island
MONTREAL R. · BRULE R. · Cheboygan
MENOMINEE R.
WISCONSIN · N. Manitou Island · Petoskey
S. Manitou Island · Alpena
LAKE HURON
Sleeping Bear Dunes National Lakeshore · Traverse City
Manistee · Higgins Lake · Houghton Lake
Houghton Lake
Harbor Beach
Midland · Bay City
Mount Pleasant · Saginaw
Milwaukee · Muskegon · Grand Rapids · Flint · Port Huron
Grand Haven · Holland · Lansing
LAKE MICHIGAN
Kalamazoo · Battle Creek · Dearborn · Detroit · Windsor
Chicago · Ann Arbor
Gary · INDIANA · OHIO · Toledo · LAKE ERIE

The Motor City
The U.S. auto industry began in Detroit and the nearby cities of Dearborn, Flint, and Lansing. When Americans began buying more foreign cars during the 1980s, the auto plants in and around Detroit suffered. Yet the area remains home to America's three largest car companies.

400 miles (644 km)

Midwest · Michigan

ABOUT MICHIGAN

NICKNAME: Wolverine State	POPULATION: 9,817,242 (8th)	FLOWER: Apple blossom
CAPITAL: Lansing	AREA: 96,705 sq. mi. (11th)	TREE: White pine
STATEHOOD: January 26, 1837 (26th)	(250,358 sq km)	BIRD: Robin
MOTTO: If you seek a beautiful peninsula, look around you.	HIGHEST POINT: 1,979 ft. (Mount Arvon) LOWEST POINT: 571 ft. (Lake Erie)	FISH: Brook trout

63

FROM THE OJIBWA WORDS *MICI GAMA*, MEANING "GREAT WATER."

Michigan

A peninsula is a spit of land, shaped like a tongue, bounded on three sides by water. The state of Michigan is actually a pair of peninsulas, one divided from the other by the Straits of Mackinac (pronounced MACK-i-naw). Michigan's sometimes hilly, sometimes swampy Upper Peninsula is connected to the flatter, mitten-shaped Lower Peninsula by the Mackinac Bridge.

Michigan is called the Great Lakes State because it borders four of the five Great Lakes. As a result, shipping has always been an important business there. The locks at Sault Ste. Marie (nicknamed "the Soo") were opened in 1855 to service ships carrying timber and iron ore from Minnesota and the Upper Peninsula. These locks, which equalize the water level between Lake Superior and Lake Huron, are still among the world's busiest.

Michiganders in great numbers also use the Great Lakes for recreation. The rural Upper Peninsula doesn't have many people, but most of them fish. So do the carloads of Detroiters and Chicagoans who visit the Upper Peninsula each summer for a vacation out-of-doors. Despite the fact that it contains every one of Michigan's major cities and important industrial centers, the Lower Peninsula is no less outdoorsy. In fact, Michiganders of both peninsulas own more boats than residents of any other state.

The fish boil has been a Great Lakes tradition since the nineteenth century. It was devised by Scandinavian immigrants who wanted an easy way to cook whitefish and lake trout. For a traditional outdoor fish boil, Michiganders cook chunks of fish, potatoes, and onions in seasoned water over large wood fires.

75%

Michigan's Slice of the Pie
Michigan produces about 75 percent of the sour pie cherries grown in the United States. The area around Traverse City is particularly good for growing cherries because Lake Michigan moderates the weather there, tempering the frosts and cooling the orchards during summer.

Large ships haul cargo from the Midwest to the East (and beyond) using the St. Lawrence Seaway. This system of canals, locks, and dams joins the Great Lakes to the Atlantic Ocean.

64

STATE FACTS
This box lists useful information about each state. The numbers in parentheses refer to that state's rank among the fifty states. *Statehood* refers to the date that a state joined the Union. The population figures, provided by the Bureau of the Census, are estimates as of July 1, 1999 (the most recent estimates can be found online at www.census.gov).

Key to Metric Abbreviations

cm	centimeters
ha	hectares
kg	kilograms
km	kilometers
l	liters
m	meters
sq km	square kilometers

How to Use This Book

There are certain questions that an atlas can answer easily. For example: What's the capital of Kansas? Or: Which interstate highway runs between San Francisco and Los Angeles? The type of maps used in the *Scholastic Atlas of the United States* present this sort of information well. However, people often ask questions about the United States that maps can't answer. For instance: How are North Carolinians different from South Carolinians? Or: What makes Minnesotans special?

To answer these much more difficult questions, people usually turn to novelists, playwrights, and humorists, rather than mapmakers. Even so, there are facts about each state—who lives in it, what the people do, what the land is like—that can help students understand more about the quality of life there. You'll find many of these facts in the pages that follow, some presented in words and others in pictures. Perhaps not all your questions will be answered, but the description of each state provided will give you a good start.

One final note: The statistics presented in this book are the most recent that were available when the book was written. Most reflect data from 1998 and 1999.

CANADA

Maine
page 12

KENNEBEC RIVER

PENOBSCOT RIVER

Vermont
page 20

CONNECTICUT RIVER

MERRIMACK RIVER

New Hampshire
page 16

Massachusetts
page 14

HOUSATONIC RIVER

Rhode Island
page 18

Connecticut
page 10

ATLANTIC OCEAN

New England

The Appalachian Mountain chain, which runs from Alabama all the way north to Canada, dominates the topography of New England. Among other ranges, the Appalachians include the Green Mountains of Vermont, the White Mountains of New Hampshire, and the Longfellow Mountains of Maine. The region's most important waterway is the Connecticut River, whose valley separates the Western New England Uplands from the slightly less hilly Eastern New England Uplands.

LEGEND

🛣 **20** Interstate Highways

⭐ State Capital

▲ Highest Point

0	miles	25
0	kilometers	40

The Insurance City

The U.S. insurance industry, which began in Connecticut, has been headquartered in Hartford for more than two hundred years. During the eighteenth century, Hartford firms insured ships and cargoes. Later, they pioneered other types of coverage, such as accident and automobile insurance.

MASSACHUSETTS

Springfield

LITCHFIELD HILLS

HOUSATONIC RIVER

SHEPAUG RIVER

NAUGATUCK RIVER

WILLIMANTIC R.

Putnam

RHODE ISLAND

QUINEBAUG RIVER

91

84

Windsor

Torrington

Hartford ⭐

Manchester

384

Willimantic

New Britain

SHETUCKET R.

Poughkeepsie

NEW YORK

84

91

Middletown

Norwich

691

Waterbury

84

Meriden

CONNECTICUT R.

THAMES R.

395

95

Candlewood Lake

91

Lake Gaillard

New London

Mystic

Danbury

New Haven

West Haven

Groton

95

684

Stratford

Milford

Bridgeport **95**

Norwalk

Long Island Sound

Stamford

Greenwich

287

New York City

ATLANTIC OCEAN

DID YOU KNOW?

that Hartford resident Mark Twain once said of the state's changeable climate, "If you don't like Connecticut weather, wait a minute?"

◄———— 90 miles (145 km) ————►

ABOUT CONNECTICUT

NICKNAME: Constitution State

CAPITAL: Hartford

STATEHOOD: January 9, 1788 (5th)

MOTTO: He who transplanted sustains.

POPULATION: 3,282,031 (29th)

AREA: 5,544 sq. mi. (48th) (14,353 sq km)

HIGHEST POINT: 2,380 ft. (Mount Frissell)

LOWEST POINT: Sea level (Long Island Sound)

FLOWER: Mountain laurel

TREE: White oak

BIRD: American robin

Connecticut

Today, most people think of Yankees as baseball players. However, when Mark Twain wrote *A Connecticut Yankee in King Arthur's Court* in 1889, he used the word *Yankee* to mean "someone from New England."

Connecticut Yankees were, for Twain, a special breed: They were tinkerers with a knack for making things. Because Connecticut can claim no oil or mineral wealth, residents have had to rely on "Yankee ingenuity" for their prosperity. Products invented in Connecticut include the revolver (by Samuel Colt in 1835), vulcanized rubber (by Charles Goodyear in 1839), and the cylinder lock (by Linus Yale in 1861). Even today, manufacturing is a crucial part of the state's economic success, especially the production of military transport equipment. Factories in Bridgeport turn out helicopters (invented in Connecticut in 1939), while highly skilled workers assemble jet engines in East Hartford and nuclear submarines in Groton.

Although the Connecticut River Valley is quite fertile, the thin, rocky soil on either side makes farming difficult. To the west, the land rises into the Litchfield Hills, where the state's highest elevations are found. On the other side of the Connecticut River, the land slopes down to the southeast. Along the state's southern border are marshy coastal lowlands that drain into Long Island Sound. This coastal plain and the Connecticut River Valley, both relatively flat, hold most of Connecticut's larger cities.

Native American Gaming
Although gambling is generally illegal in Connecticut, the state contains two of the world's largest casinos: the Mohegan Sun and Foxwoods, both near New London. These casinos are allowed to operate because they belong to Native American groups, which are treated legally as independent nations existing within the United States.

Wrap It Up
What little agriculture Connecticut does have involves mostly direct-to-market products, such as flowering plants, fresh vegetables, and Christmas trees. The one important exception is shade-grown tobacco leaf. The best Connecticut River Valley leaves, about twenty-four inches (61 cm) long, are used to wrap cigars.

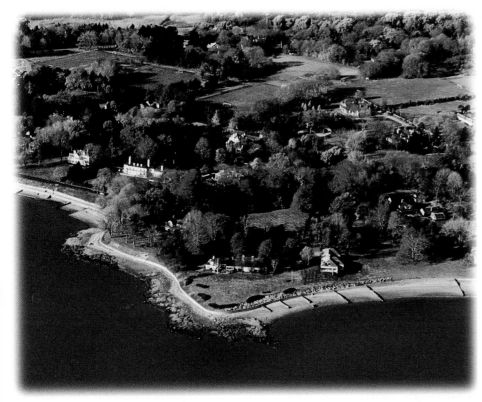

Judging by per-capita income, Connecticut is the nation's richest state. Its wealthiest area, Fairfield County, nearly borders New York City. Residents there include many well-paid corporate executives who commute to jobs in Manhattan.

LEGEND

🛣 20 Interstate Highways	⭐ State Capital	🟥 National Parks and Refuges	🌲 National Forests	🔺 Highest Point	0 ⸺ miles ⸺ 50 / 0 ⸺ kilometers ⸺ 80

Parlez Vous?

There are no minorities to speak of in Maine, which is 98 percent white. However, many of those whites are transplanted French Canadians for whom English is a second language. Much of Maine is bilingual, and in the St. John River Valley, French is the dominant tongue.

DID YOU KNOW?

that the 2,034-mile-long (3,273-kilometer-long) Appalachian Trail ends at Mount Katahdin, Maine's highest point? Because of its height, Mount Katahdin is also the first place that the sun strikes the continental United States.

⟵⸺ 207 miles (333 km) ⸺⟶

ABOUT MAINE

NICKNAME: Pine Tree State
CAPITAL: Augusta
STATEHOOD: March 15, 1820 (23rd)
MOTTO: I direct.

POPULATION: 1,253,040 (39th)
AREA: 35,387 sq. mi. (39th)
(91,613 sq km)
HIGHEST POINT: 5,267 ft. (Mount Katahdin)
LOWEST POINT: Sea level (Atlantic Ocean)

FLOWER: White pinecone and tasse
TREE: White pine
BIRD: Chickadee
FISH: Landlocked salmon

Maine

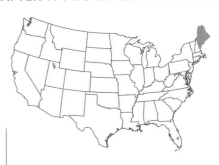

Maine is large, with about as much land as the rest of New England combined. It's also roomy, with a population only slightly larger than that of Rhode Island. In fact, Maine is the least densely populated state east of the Mississippi River. This is especially true north of Bangor, where the terrain becomes mountainous, heavily forested, and sometimes impassable.

That's why most Mainers live in towns along one of the state's tidal rivers or in fishing villages along the Atlantic coast. In the north, most Mainers earn their livings from the timber industry, while in the south, tourism pays most of the bills. The southern coast from Kittery to Casco Bay is particularly popular with vacationers, who rent houses during the summer months to enjoy Maine's scenic beauty. (The ocean water is usually too cold for swimming.)

In addition to their skill at trapping lobsters and making leather goods, native Mainers are known for their restrained manner, industriousness, and endurance. The state's physical environment is harsh, with long, bitter winters and a challenging landscape. Yet stubbornness and perseverance in response to their environment have given the people of Maine a national reputation and cultural importance well beyond their economic and political status.

Maine's generally poor soil supports very little agriculture. That's not the case in Aroostook County, however, where potato farms compete with those in Idaho. Income from potatoes is so important to northeastern Maine that schools regularly excuse students so they can help out with the fall harvest.

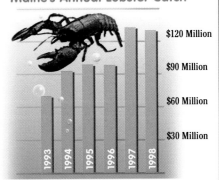

Maine's Annual Lobster Catch

$120 Million
$90 Million
$60 Million
$30 Million

1993 1994 1995 1996 1997 1998

Fishing has long been an important part of the Maine economy, and lobsters, which flourish in the state's cool coastal waters, remain the most valuable catch. However, rising prices have encouraged overfishing, and ecologists now worry that the future of the Maine lobster could be threatened.

During the last Ice Age, glaciers carved Maine's rocky shoreline into scenic cliffs, bays, coves, and beaches. Maine's numerous offshore islands are mostly the tops of hills submerged when those glaciers melted and the sea level rose.

13

LEGEND

Interstate Highways	State Capital	National Parks and Refuges	Marshlands	Highest Point	0 miles 25 0 kilometers 40

DID YOU KNOW?

that there's a Lake Chargoggagoggmanchauggauggag-oggchaubunagungamaugg near Worcester? Its Native American name means "You fish on your side; I fish on my side; nobody fishes in the middle."

The Cultural Berkshires

Many prominent music and dance groups perform in the Berkshires during the summer. The Boston Symphony Orchestra, for example, has been performing at Tanglewood, near Lenox, since 1936. In nearby Lee, the Jacob's Pillow Dance Festival features traditional and modern dance as well as ballet.

190 miles (306 km)

ABOUT MASSACHUSETTS

NICKNAME: Bay State

CAPITAL: Boston

STATEHOOD: February 6, 1788 (6th)

MOTTO: By the sword we seek peace, but peace only under liberty.

POPULATION: 6,175,169 (13th)

AREA: 10,555 sq. mi. (44th) (27,326 sq km)

HIGHEST POINT: 3,487 ft. (Mount Greylock)

LOWEST POINT: Sea level (Atlantic Ocean)

FLOWER: Mayflower

TREE: American elm

BIRD: Chickadee

FISH: Cod

Massachusetts

When people talk about the United States as a "melting pot" of different cultures, Massachusetts provides a ready example. Although Yankee Protestants dominated the colony for two hundred years, the textile mills that opened near Boston during the nineteenth century attracted a flood of immigrants. First came the Irish, then the French Canadians, then the Italians and other Europeans. The textile mills are gone now, but Massachusetts remains a top manufacturing state, with a population that's still ethnically diverse.

New Bedford, for example, contains the largest community of Portuguese Americans. The great-great-grandfathers of these people came to America to work in the whaling industry. Now many of their descendants work as commercial fishermen and in fish-processing plants. On the other hand, Boston is an Irish town, famous for its long string of Irish mayors. Of course, it's also the financial capital of New England, as well as the region's population center. Massachusetts has nearly as many residents as the other five New England states combined, and half these people live in the Boston area.

Along with the rest of the Massachusetts coastline, Boston sits on the sandy Atlantic Coastal Plain. Inland, the land rises slowly into the rocky New England Uplands. The fertile Connecticut River Valley, which divides the state, separates the southern fringe of the White Mountains (in the east) from the Berkshire Hills (in the west).

Silicon Valley East
Among the most successful businesses in Massachusetts are the technology firms lining Route 128 west of Boston. These companies have taken particular advantage of the high-tech workforce being created by such local (yet nationally prominent) universities as Harvard and the Massachusetts Institute of Technology.

GLACIER

Terminal Moraine

Martha's Vineyard

Nantucket

Cape Cod

End of the Line
Cape Cod, a sandy peninsula sixty-five miles (105 km) long, is what geologists call a terminal moraine. It marks the farthest point reached by the glacier that carved out the Connecticut River Valley. It's also the line along which the melting glacier deposited all the rocky debris it had been carrying.

Cranberries grow in bogs, or areas of wet spongy ground, that are usually flooded at harvesttime. Although the state's generally poor soil supports little agriculture, the cranberry bogs of southeastern Massachusetts produce nearly 40 percent of the nation's crop.

Interstate Highways   State Capital   National Parks and Refuges   National Forests   Highest Point

0 miles 25
0 miles 40

Although most people think of New Hampshire as primarily rural, it contains significant manufacturing. The most heavily industrialized area is Manchester, New Hampshire's largest city, where factories make machinery, computers, military communications equipment, and plastics.

DID YOU KNOW?

that New Hampshire's state representatives, who are paid just one hundred dollars a year, haven't gotten a raise since 1784?

CANADA

HALLS STREAM

Connecticut Lakes

ANDROSCOGGIN R.

Umbagog Lake

Berlin

St. Johnsbury

Littleton

MAINE

WHITE MOUNTAINS

93

Conway

VERMONT

Plymouth

Squam Lake

Hanover

Newfound Lake

Lake Winnipesaukee

Lebanon

Laconia

Portland

Great East Lake

Sunapee Lake

Franklin

SALMON FALLS RIVER

MERRIMACK RIVER

89

Claremont

Rochester

CONNECTICUT RIVER

Dover

PISCATAQUA RIVER

★ Concord

93

Portsmouth

Keene

Manchester

Exeter

ATLANTIC OCEAN

95

Derry

EXETER RIVER

Brattleboro

Wapack National Wildlife Refuge

Nashua

Lowell

MASSACHUSETTS

93

◄———————— 93 miles (150 km) ————————►

ABOUT NEW HAMPSHIRE

NICKNAME: Granite State
CAPITAL: Concord
STATEHOOD: June 21, 1788 (9th)
MOTTO: Live free or die.

POPULATION: 1,201,134 (41st)
AREA: 9,351 sq. mi. (46th) (24,209 sq km)
HIGHEST POINT: 6,288 ft. (Mount Washington)
LOWEST POINT: Sea level (Atlantic Ocean)

FLOWER: Purple lilac
TREE: White birch
BIRD: Purple finch
FISH: Brook trout, striped bass

New Hampshire

In many ways, the residents of New Hampshire are tied to the past, to an older tradition of how people's lives should be run. Although most Americans have little contact with their local governments, towns in New Hampshire still hold open meetings to decide important public issues. In fact, more than most voters, the people of New Hampshire believe in exercising their political voices. This is particularly true every four years when the state hosts its traditional "first in the nation" presidential primary.

In northern New Hampshire, where the stony White Mountains dominate the landscape, most people live in small towns that depend on lumber for their livelihood. Like Connecticut, it's a place of enduring Yankee values, where the highly conservative residents (nearly all of whom are white) are often compared to the granite bedrock underlying the state. The only industrial center is Berlin, where large mills process trees into paper and wood pulp.

South of the White Mountains, however, New Hampshire contains a number of large urban centers that house about 85 percent of the state's population. People originally concentrated in these cities because southern New Hampshire is highly industrialized. Lately, however, more and more people have been moving from Boston to nearby New Hampshire to escape the city and Massachusetts state taxes. New Hampshire has neither an income tax nor a sales tax.

Every year on the first Tuesday in March, citizens of New Hampshire take part in a tradition dating back to colonial times: the town meeting. Before the spring thaw comes and mud makes some roads impassable, town residents gather to vote on school budgets, property taxes, and other government matters.

Top Wind Speed: 231 miles per hour (372 km/hr)

The Windiest Place on Earth
Atop Mount Washington, the highest peak in New England, the National Weather Service operates a climate research station. On April 12, 1934, this station's instruments registered a world-record wind speed of 231 miles per hour. Normally, winter gusts on Mount Washington range from 120 to 160 miles (193 to 257 km) per hour.

In a Native American language once spoken in New Hampshire, *monadnock* means "mountain that stands alone." More recently, Mount Monadnock near Keene has given its name to isolated plugs of granite that become mountains once the surrounding land has eroded away.

During the late nineteenth century, Newport was perhaps the world's most fashionable resort. The richest Americans built summer "cottages" there along the famous Newport Cliff Walk. The grandest of these mansions is the seventy-room Breakers, built by the Vanderbilt family in 1892.

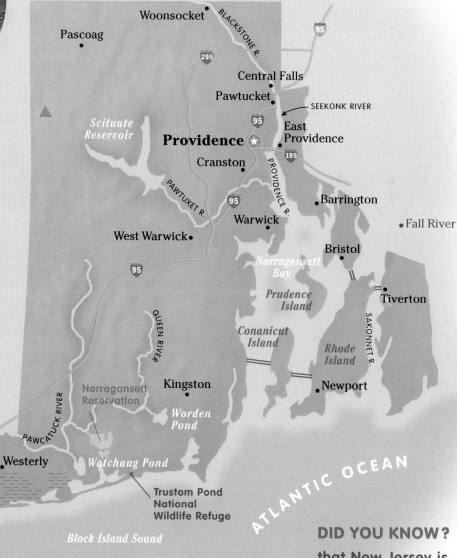

MASSACHUSETTS

Woonsocket
BLACKSTONE R.
95
Pascoag
295
Central Falls
Pawtucket
SEEKONK RIVER
Scituate Reservoir
95
East Providence
Providence ★
195
Cranston
PROVIDENCE R.
PAWTUXET R.
Barrington
95
Warwick
Fall River
West Warwick
Bristol
Narragansett Bay
Prudence Island
Conanicut Island
Tiverton
SAKONNET R.
95
Rhode Island
QUEEN RIVER
Narragansett Reservation
Kingston
Newport
PAWCATUCK RIVER
Worden Pond
CONNECTICUT
Westerly
Watchaug Pond
Trustom Pond National Wildlife Refuge
ATLANTIC OCEAN
Block Island Sound
Block Island

DID YOU KNOW?
that New Jersey is the only state more densely populated than Rhode Island?

◄—— 37 miles (60 km) ——►

ABOUT RHODE ISLAND

NICKNAME: Ocean State	**POPULATION:** 990,819 (43rd)	**FLOWER:** Violet
CAPITAL: Providence	**AREA:** 1,545 sq. mi. (50th)	**TREE:** Red maple
STATEHOOD: May 29, 1790 (13th)	(4,000 sq km)	**BIRD:** Rhode Island red
MOTTO: Hope.	**HIGHEST POINT:** 812 ft. (Jerimoth Hill)	
	LOWEST POINT: Sea level (Atlantic Ocean)	

Rhode Island

Because Rhode Island is the smallest state, it's particularly easy for Rhode Islanders to travel—that is, they don't have to go very far to reach Massachusetts or Connecticut. Yet people there will tell you that Rhode Islanders like to stay close to home. Part of the reason is that they're proud of where they live, even though there's so little of it.

Since the founding of the colony by Protestant dissidents in 1636, Rhode Islanders have championed religious tolerance. Those who have benefited include Jews, who in 1763 established the first U.S. synagogue in Newport, and Roman Catholics, who immigrated to the state in large numbers once Rhode Island began to industrialize during the nineteenth century.

The state had little choice but to industrialize. Because of its poor soil, agriculture wasn't an option. So, relying on their reputation for fine craftsmanship, Rhode Islanders built factories instead. These factories, in turn, attracted workers from other countries who diversified the mostly white, mostly Protestant population. Today, Rhode Island has a higher percentage of Roman Catholics than any other state, with large Irish and Italian communities in Providence and French Canadians in Woonsocket.

The island for which the state is named is the largest of thirty-five in Narragansett Bay, where sand beaches and salt marshes dominate the terrain. On the mainland, however, the lowlands of the Atlantic Coastal Plain quickly give way to the low, rocky hills of the New England Uplands.

Factories in Providence began making costume jewelry in 1794, and the city remains a national leader in the field. Designed to be trendy and disposable, these fashion accessories are affordable because they're made from inexpensive materials rather than precious metals and gemstones.

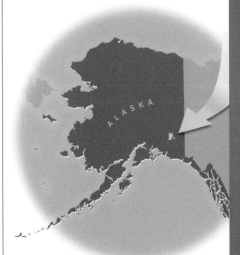

A Tiny Fraction of the Size
Rhode Island is so small that it would take 425 Rhode Islands to fill up just one Alaska, the largest of the fifty states.

Although freighters use it to reach the busy port of Providence, Narragansett Bay is best known for its water sports. In particular, it's the focus of yachting on the Atlantic coast.

LEGEND

Interstate Highways | **State Capital** | **National Forests** | **Highest Point**

| 0 | miles | 25 |
| 0 | kilometers | 40 |

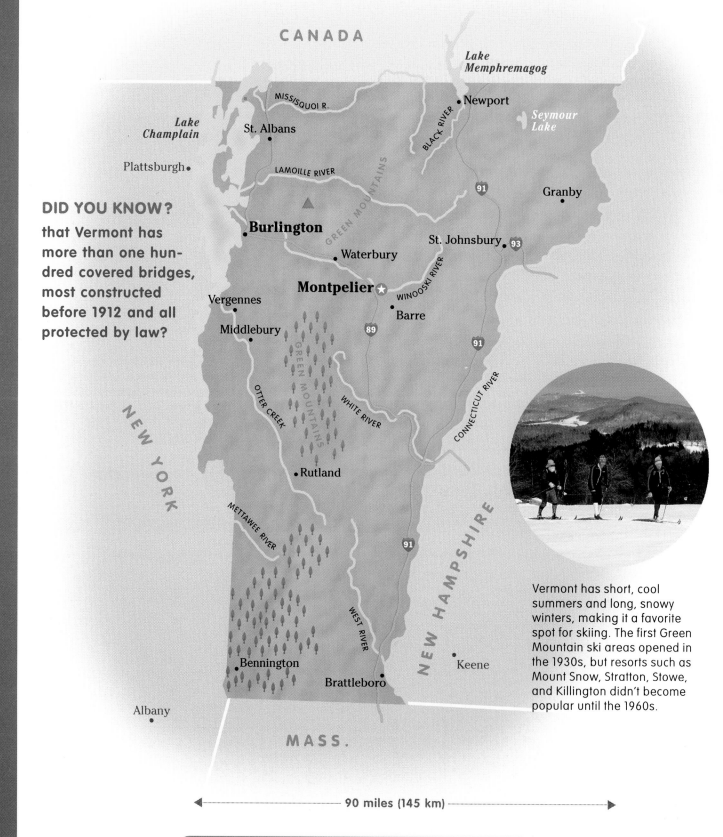

CANADA

Lake Memphremagog

MISSISQUOI R.

Lake Champlain

St. Albans

Newport

BLACK RIVER

Seymour Lake

Plattsburgh

LAMOILLE RIVER

91

Granby

GREEN MOUNTAINS

DID YOU KNOW?
that Vermont has more than one hundred covered bridges, most constructed before 1912 and all protected by law?

Burlington

Waterbury

St. Johnsbury

93

Montpelier ☆

WINOOSKI RIVER

Vergennes

Barre

Middlebury

89

91

OTTER CREEK

GREEN MOUNTAINS

WHITE RIVER

CONNECTICUT RIVER

NEW YORK

Rutland

METTAWEE RIVER

91

NEW HAMPSHIRE

WEST RIVER

Bennington

Keene

Brattleboro

Albany

Vermont has short, cool summers and long, snowy winters, making it a favorite spot for skiing. The first Green Mountain ski areas opened in the 1930s, but resorts such as Mount Snow, Stratton, Stowe, and Killington didn't become popular until the 1960s.

MASS.

⟵————— 90 miles (145 km) —————⟶

ABOUT VERMONT

NICKNAME: Green Mountain State

CAPITAL: Montpelier

STATEHOOD: March 4, 1791 (14th)

MOTTO: Freedom and unity.

POPULATION: 593,740 (49th)

AREA: 9,615 sq. mi. (45th)
(24,892 sq km)

HIGHEST POINT: 4,393 ft. (Mount Mansfield)

LOWEST POINT: 95 ft. (Lake Champlain)

FLOWER: Red clover

TREE: Sugar maple

BIRD: Hermit thrush

FISH: Brook trout, walleye pike

Vermont

Like Iowa, Vermont is a small-town state. Montpelier, the smallest state capital, contains just eight thousand people, and Vermont's other cities aren't much larger. In fact, about as many people live in Boston as live in all of Vermont. Even the state's factories are small: Four out of five employ fewer than fifty people.

As late as the 1950s, the typical Vermonter was a Protestant of English descent, and the state is still 99 percent white. Following the social upheaval of the 1960s, however, many young people moved to Vermont, hoping for a simpler, more natural lifestyle. One result of this influx (and the new sensibility brought by these people) has been the development of a new specialty food market in the state. Products such as goat cheese, organic vegetables, and emu burgers now proudly bear the "Made in Vermont" label.

Like its neighbors, Vermont is mountainous, yet unlike the other New England states, Vermont depends heavily on agriculture. Crops aren't very profitable, because only the Connecticut River Valley has suitable soil, so most Vermont farmers raise livestock instead. Dairy cows happily graze on most mountainsides, producing the milk used to make Vermont's famous cheddar cheese.

The heavily forested Green Mountains that give Vermont its name are the backbone of the state, running north to south in a band about thirty miles (50 km) wide. The rest of the state is mostly hill country cut by fast-flowing streams.

Milk accounts for about three quarters of Vermont's farm income. Traditionally that milk has gone to make cheddar cheese. However, some of it now goes to the Ben & Jerry's ice cream factory in Waterbury. With flavors such as Rainforest Crunch and Cherry Garcia, founders Ben Cohen and Jerry Greenfield have used 1960s sensibilities to promote their product.

Vermont leads the nation in maple syrup production, which the locals call sugaring. Maple sap begins to flow in early spring, when daytime temperatures first rise above 40°F (5°C) yet nighttime temperatures remain below freezing. Sugarmakers boil down the sap from four trees, about forty gallons (150 l), to make a single gallon (3.8 l) of syrup.

Poet Robert Frost once described fall in the Green Mountains as a time when the "leaves go to glory." About three out of every four Vermonters live either on farms or in small towns like this one.

CANADA

LAKE ONTARIO

LAKE ERIE

ERIE CANAL

New York
page 30

MOHAWK RIVER

HUDSON RIVER

ALLEGHENY RIVER

Pennsylvania
page 32

SUSQUEHANNA RIVER

DELAWARE RIVER

OHIO RIVER

New
Jersey
page 28

MONONGAHELA RIVER

Maryland
page 26

POTOMAC RIVER

Delaware
page 24

Washington,
D.C.
page 34

ATLANTIC OCEAN

E very Mid-Atlantic state sits—at least in some small part—on both the Piedmont Plateau and the Atlantic Coastal Plain. The line along which these two regions meet is called the fall line because the land there drops sharply. Two hundred years ago, George Washington chose the point at which the fall line crosses the Potomac River for the location of his new federal city. Hikers today can easily tell when they're near the fall line because of all the rapids and waterfalls it creates.

Mid-Atlantic

PENNSYLVANIA

Philadelphia •

BRANDYWINE CREEK

95

295

Claymont

Elsmere

Wilmington

Newark

95

New Castle

CHRISTINA R.

CHESAPEAKE & DELAWARE CANAL

DELAWARE RIVER

Middletown

NEW JERSEY

Smyrna

LEIPSIC R.

Dover ☆

Bombay Hook National Wildlife Refuge

Delaware Bay

MARYLAND

Milford

Prime Hook National Wildlife Refuge

MISPILLION R.

Lewes

Rehoboth Beach

Georgetown

Rehoboth Bay

Seaford

Millsboro

Indian River Bay

NANTICOKE RIVER

Bethany Beach

Cypress Swamp

ATLANTIC OCEAN

Ocean City •

By far Delaware's most important corporation is chemical manufacturer E.I. du Pont de Nemours & Co. A French immigrant founded the company in 1802, when he built a gunpowder mill along the Brandywine Creek near Wilmington. Now Delaware's largest employer, Du Pont operates ten chemical plants in the state.

DID YOU KNOW?

that a single town, Millsboro, holds the records for Delaware's highest and lowest temperatures: 110°F (43°C) in 1930 and -17°F (-27°C) in 1893?

←------ 35 miles (56 km) ------→

ABOUT DELAWARE

NICKNAME: First State

CAPITAL: Dover

STATEHOOD: December 7, 1787 (1st)

MOTTO: Liberty and independence.

POPULATION: 753,538 (45th)

AREA: 2,489 sq. mi. (49th)
(6,444 sq km)

HIGHEST POINT: 448 ft. (Ebright Road)

LOWEST POINT: Sea level (Atlantic Ocean)

FLOWER: Peach blossom

TREE: American holly

BIRD: Blue hen chicken

FISH: Weakfish

Delaware

DECEMBER 7, 1787

In Delaware, everyone seems to know everyone else. Of course that's not literally true, yet the state is small enough that its residents cross paths often. Because of this, Delaware is the sort of place where much business gets done in restaurants and on golf courses.

After chemicals—that is, after Du Pont—Delaware's biggest business is incorporation. Of the five hundred largest U.S. companies, more than half are Delaware corporations. This may seem odd for such a small state, but Delaware has been passing laws to attract corporations since 1899. Although nearly all these companies do business elsewhere, they've incorporated in Delaware because of the state's low taxation, up-to-date laws, and experienced judges. In return, they provide work for armies of lawyers, accountants, and other business professionals familiar with the state's legal requirements and procedures. Overall, corporate taxes and fees make up more than one fifth of Delaware's total revenue.

Delaware sits on the Delmarva Peninsula, which separates the Chesapeake Bay from the Atlantic Ocean. The Chesapeake & Delaware Canal, linking these two bodies of water, provides an important boundary between the state's industrial north and its agricultural south. Northern Delaware contains about two thirds of the state's population and all of its major transportation routes, while the main industry in the south is chicken farming.

The Brandywine Valley north of Wilmington is called Chateau Country because of its many Du Pont family mansions. Two have become museums: Winterthur (pictured above) houses the nation's finest collection of early American decorative arts, while the Hagley Museum, on the site of the original Du Pont powder works, documents life during the nineteenth century.

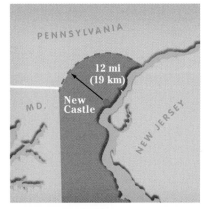

PENNSYLVANIA

12 mi (19 km)

M D.

New Castle

NEW JERSEY

Delaware is the only state with a partially rounded border, the result of a land dispute during the early 1680s. At that time, William Penn and the Duke of York agreed that the boundary between Pennsylvania and Delaware would be an arc "drawn at twelve miles' distance from New Castle."

The salt marshes and estuaries that line Delaware Bay provide excellent habitats for birds and shellfish. Delaware's strict shoreline protection laws, the first of their kind in the nation, forbid pollution-causing factories too close to the bay.

DID YOU KNOW?

that a Baltimore law makes it illegal to take a lion to the movies?

PENNSYLVANIA

Philadelphia •

Wilmington •

Elkton •

Hagerstown   Westminster   Bel Air   Aberdeen

Cumberland

Deep Creek Lake

ALLEGHENY MOUNTAINS

Liberty Reservoir

Frederick

Baltimore

Dundalk

CHESTER R.

DELAWARE

WEST VIRGINIA

POTOMAC RIVER

Columbia

Wheaton

Rockville

Silver Spring

Washington, D.C.   Bowie   **Annapolis**

VIRGINIA

CHOPTANK R.

Easton •

Blackwater National Wildlife Refuge

Cambridge •

NANTICOKE R.

Salisbury •

Ocean City •

PATUXENT RIVER

During the late 1980s, Baltimore energetically renovated its downtown Inner Harbor area. The centerpiece was a hundred-million-dollar ballpark: Oriole Park at Camden Yards. The success of this old-style brick baseball stadium—nearly every game is sold out—has inspired other cities, such as Cleveland and Denver, to build their own downtown ballparks.

• Richmond

Chesapeake Bay

Assateague Island National Seashore

ATLANTIC OCEAN

195 miles (314 km)

ABOUT MARYLAND

NICKNAME: Old Line State

CAPITAL: Annapolis

STATEHOOD: April 28, 1788 (7th)

MOTTO: Manly deeds, womanly words.

POPULATION: 5,171,634 (19th)

AREA: 12,407 sq. mi. (42nd) (32,120 sq km)

HIGHEST POINT: 3,360 ft. (Backbone Mt.)

LOWEST POINT: Sea level (Atlantic Ocean)

FLOWER: Black-eyed Susan

TREE: White oak

BIRD: Baltimore oriole

FISH: Rockfish

Maryland

Maryland has so many different looks that what you see depends on what you're looking for. If you're looking for people, you'll find most of them living between Washington, D.C., and Baltimore. Three out of every four Marylanders live in this densely populated corridor because most of the jobs are there. The leading industries are electrical equipment and food processing, but the federal government is also a major employer. Many Marylanders commute to jobs in D.C., but even more work at federal facilities in Maryland.

If you're looking for land, you'll find that most of the state is rural. On Maryland's Eastern Shore, part of the Atlantic Coastal Plain, farmers raise broiler chickens inland while resort towns line the Atlantic beaches. In western Maryland, atop the hilly Piedmont, fertile farmland is occasionally interrupted by large belts of clay. (This clay provided the raw material for the bricks that have made Maryland's homes and factories so distinctive.) Farther west, in the section of the state called the "bird's wing" because of its odd shape, the land rises sharply into the Allegheny Mountains.

Finally, even if you're not looking for water, you'll find it impossible to miss Chesapeake Bay, the largest estuary in the United States. The bay was formed at the end of the last Ice Age when rising seawaters flooded the southern Susquehanna River Valley. Today it's 193 miles (311 km) long with 3,200 miles (5,200 km) of shoreline.

Maryland's older industrial look often appeals to feature filmmakers in search of colorful urban locations. Among the first directors to shoot films in Baltimore were home-grown talents Barry Levinson (*Diner*, *Avalon*) and John Waters (*Hairspray*, *Cry-Baby*). The city now expects to host two or three major productions each year.

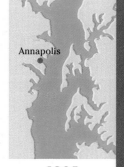

1795   **1995**

Shifting Shoreline
Maryland's shoreline has been frustrating mapmakers for centuries. The problem is that the tidal waters of Chesapeake Bay keep rearranging the land, filling in swamps as they wash away islands.

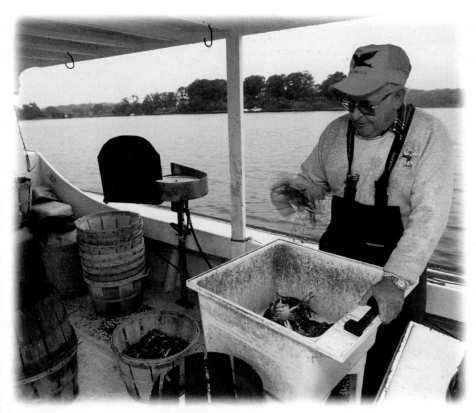

Although pollution and overfishing have dramatically reduced the oyster and striped bass populations, Chesapeake Bay still produces about five hundred million pounds (227 million kg) of seafood each year, including one hundred million pounds (45 million kg) of blue crabs.

LEGEND

🛣️ **20**	⭐	⬛	░░░	🔺	0	miles 25
Interstate Highways	State Capital	National Parks and Refuges	Marshlands	Highest Point	0	kilometers 40

New Jersey has one of the busiest and most extensive transportation systems in the world. The trucking, shipping, and air routes that converge at Newark make use of the New Jersey Turnpike (the busiest U.S. toll road), the Port of Newark, and Newark Airport.

NEW YORK

KITTATINNY MTS.

Greenwood Lake

Wanaque Reservoir

Lake Hopatcong

80

Paterson

Dover

Clifton

Hoboken

New York City

HUDSON RIVER

95

287

Newark

Jersey City

Elizabeth

Bayonne

78

Plainfield

278

DELAWARE RIVER

Edison

Perth Amboy

RARITAN RIVER

Princeton

Red Bank

Long Branch

95

Asbury Park

PENNSYLVANIA

⭐ **Trenton**

95

195

295

Philadelphia

76

New Jersey Turnpike

Camden

Cherry Hill

PINE BARRENS

Garden State Parkway

ATLANTIC OCEAN

Wilmington

295

MULLICA RIVER

GREAT EGG HARBOR RIVER

Vineland

Edwin B. Forsythe National Wildlife Refuge

MAURICE RIVER

Atlantic City

DELAWARE

Delaware Bay

Cape May

DID YOU KNOW?

that it's illegal to pump your own gasoline at service stations in New Jersey?

57 miles (92 km)

ABOUT NEW JERSEY

NICKNAME: Garden State

CAPITAL: Trenton

STATEHOOD: December 18, 1787 (3rd)

MOTTO: Liberty and prosperity.

POPULATION: 8,143,412 (9th)

AREA: 8,722 sq. mi. (47th)
(22,580 sq km)

HIGHEST POINT: 1,803 ft. (High Point)

LOWEST POINT: Sea level (Atlantic Ocean)

FLOWER: Purple violet

TREE: Red oak

BIRD: Eastern goldfinch

New Jersey

Benjamin Franklin once described New Jersey as "a cider barrel tapped at both ends." He was referring to the fact that in colonial times New Jersey grew much of the food eaten in both New York City and Philadelphia. Two hundred years later, the state has changed, having transformed itself into an industrial powerhouse. Yet many people still describe it incorrectly as a collection of highway exits between Times Square and Independence Hall.

It's certainly true that many New Jerseyans live in suburbs and commute to jobs in New York City and Philadelphia. Yet New Jersey has a prosperous economy of its own. For instance, it leads the nation in pharmaceutical drug production and trails only Texas in chemical production. In addition, New Jersey boasts a number of important industrial research facilities, a tradition begun by Thomas Edison in 1876 when he built the first U.S. research laboratory in Menlo Park. Because of all this heavy industry, though, New Jersey has paid a steep price in toxic waste and environmental pollution.

Ironically, because so many New Jerseyans live packed into suburbs, two thirds of the state is open land. In southern and eastern Jersey, this land is dominated by the Pine Barrens, a region of infertile soil sitting atop the Cohansey Aquifer, which is believed to hold the largest supply of freshwater in the Northeast.

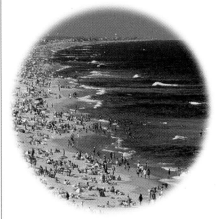

The Jersey Shore begins at Cape May, the nation's first summer resort. A short drive north is Atlantic City, the home of the Miss America pageant since 1921 and legalized gambling since 1978. Closer to New York City are the beach towns made famous by Bruce Springsteen, who grew up near Asbury Park.

Among the states, New Jersey has the ninth largest population and the fourth smallest area. This means that a lot of New Jerseyans live in a relatively small space. As a result, New Jersey has the highest population density in the United States, with more people per square mile than India or Japan.

New Jersey's nickname is the Garden State because of its many truck farms. These small farms produce fresh vegetables, milk, and eggs that are shipped by truck to New York City and Philadelphia.

Interstate Highways

State Capital

Native American Reservations

National Forests

Highest Point

| 0 | | miles | | 50 |
| 0 | | kilometers | | 80 |

New York City is the hub of many industries, including fashion, theater, art, broadcasting, publishing, advertising, public relations, and financial services. New York City's financial community is collectively known as Wall Street because the New York Stock Exchange is located there.

ST. LAWRENCE RIVER

St. Regis Reservation

Lake Champlain

Ogdensburg

Potsdam

Plattsburgh

Lake Placid

Burlington

CANADA

RAQUETTE R.

Watertown

ADIRONDACK MTS

87

VERMONT

81

LAKE ONTARIO

Oswego

Oneida Lake

Rome

Great Sacandaga Lake

METTAWEE RIVER

Lake George

Glens Falls

ERIE CANAL

NIAGARA R.

Niagara Falls

Rochester

Utica

90

MOHAWK RIVER

Schenectady

Buffalo

Syracuse

Geneva

GENESEE RIVER

90

L. ERIE

90

390

Finger Lakes

Ithaca

Oneonta

88

Albany

Troy

90

MASS.

Cattaraugus Reservation

Jamestown

ALLEGHENY R.

Corning

Elmira

SUSQUEHANNA R.

Binghamton

81

CATSKILL MTS

Ashokan Reservoir

HUDSON RIVER

Allegany Reservation

81

DELAWARE R.

Kingston

87

Poughkeepsie

CONN.

PENNSYLVANIA

Scranton

Middletown

Newburgh

84

684

95

Long Island Sound

DID YOU KNOW?

that in 1644 the governor of New York (then New Amsterdam) noted eighteen languages being spoken by the colony's inhabitants?

Yonkers

New York City

Allentown

N.J.

Trenton

Levittown

Hempstead

278

495

Riverhead

ATLANTIC OCEAN

320 miles (515 km)

ABOUT NEW YORK

NICKNAME: Empire State

CAPITAL: Albany

STATEHOOD: July 26, 1788 (11th)

MOTTO: Ever upward.

POPULATION: 18,196,601 (3rd)

AREA: 54,471 sq. mi. (27th)
(141,019 sq km)

HIGHEST POINT: 5,344 ft. (Mount Marcy)

LOWEST POINT: Sea level (Atlantic Ocean)

FLOWER: Rose

TREE: Sugar maple

BIRD: Bluebird

FISH: Brook trout

New York

Until the late 1960s, New York led the nation in nearly every economic, population, and cultural category. Now it ranks third in population and seventh in manufacturing jobs. New York's economic decline has particularly troubled upstate cities such as Buffalo and Rochester, which have lost thousands of high-paying industrial jobs. On the other hand, New York City remains essentially unchanged: It continues to be an international cultural center, the home of the world's most important financial markets, and the headquarters of more major corporations than anyplace else on earth.

As in Illinois, a clear distinction exists between residents of "the City" and the rest of the state's population. Manhattanites tend to think of upstate New York as one large cow pasture, while many upstaters consider New York City a potentially dangerous foreign land. In fact, a remarkable number of languages is spoken in New York City, which has long been an important point of entry for immigrants.

Just as New York's people and economy are highly diverse, so is its geography. The only state to border both the Atlantic Ocean and the Great Lakes, it encompasses nine topographical regions, most created by glaciers during the last Ice Age. New York's two major mountain ranges are the Catskills and the Adirondacks. The Adirondacks are particularly notable because the state has set aside a large part of these rugged, sparsely populated mountains as a wilderness preserve.

The Melting Pot
Although most cities in New York have varied populations, none compares with New York City for its racial and ethnic mix. For instance, in the New York City metropolitan area, there are significant populations of Puerto Ricans, Haitians, Dominicans, Jews, and Chinese. In addition, there are more blacks in New York than in any other state.

Buffalo gets more attention, but Syracuse is actually the snowiest U.S. city outside Alaska, with a mean annual snowfall of 110.1 inches (279.7 cm). The reason is the lake effect. As air moves west, it soaks up moisture over the Great Lakes. When this air reaches land and cools down, excess moisture is squeezed out as snow.

In the Hudson River Valley, although apples are an important crop, milk is the leading agricultural product. Statewide, dairy products account for about half of all farm income.

Interstate Highways | State Capital | National Parks and Refuges | National Forests | Highest Point

| 0 | miles | 50 |
| 0 | kilometers | 80 |

DID YOU KNOW?
that Pittsburgh's steel factories once produced so much smoke that motorists had to use headlights during the day?

LAKE ERIE

NEW YORK

Erie • 90

Erie National Wildlife Refuge

Binghamton •

Bradford •

Pymatuning Reservoir

ALLEGHENY RIVER

Oil City •

Scranton •
Lake Wallen-paupack

81

380

DELAWARE RIVER

84

OHIO

90

79

80

Youngstown •

New Castle •
Butler •

WEST BRANCH SUSQUEHANNA R.

Williamsport •

Wilkes-Barre •

80

Hazleton •

80

76

N.J.

State College •

ALLEGHENY MTS.

80

180

81

Pottsville •

Bethlehem •

78

Allentown

76

OHIO R.

76

Pittsburgh

Altoona •

JUNIATA R.

Harrisburg ★

Hershey •

Reading •

SCHUYLKILL R.

Trenton •

Johnstown •

Raystown Lake

Lancaster

Philadelphia •

95

Greensburg •

99

76

MONONGAHELA R.

70

70

79

Carlisle •

Chambersburg •

York •

70

81

83

95

Chester •
Wilmington •

W.VA.

VA.

MARYLAND

Baltimore •

DEL.

Lancaster County in the heart of Pennsylvania Dutch country has a high concentration of dairy farms. That's why Milton Hershey chose to locate his milk chocolate business there. Since Hershey's factory opened in 1905, it has grown to become the world's largest chocolate plant.

307 miles (494 km)

ABOUT PENNSYLVANIA

NICKNAME: Keystone State
CAPITAL: Harrisburg
STATEHOOD: December 12, 1787 (2nd)
MOTTO: Virtue, liberty, and independence.

POPULATION: 11,994,016 (6th)
AREA: 46,058 sq. mi. (33rd) (119,239 sq km)
HIGHEST POINT: 3,213 ft. (Mount Davis)
LOWEST POINT: Sea level (Delaware River)

FLOWER: Mountain laurel
TREE: Hemlock
BIRD: Ruffed grouse
FISH: Brook trout

Pennsylvania

Like neighboring West Virginia, Pennsylvania is a coal state. Its plentiful energy resources once fueled major steel factories in Pittsburgh, Allentown, and elsewhere. Now with most of those mills closed, the air is cleaner, but some local economies have yet to recover.

Easing that economic burden has been the state's robust food-processing industry. Pennsylvania leads the nation in the production of snack foods, especially potato chips, pretzels, and chocolate. It also ranks fourth in milk production and fourth in ice cream making.

With so much agriculture, it's easy to understand why Pennsylvania has been described as "Philadelphia at one end, Pittsburgh at the other, and Alabama in the middle." In other words, despite containing the fifth and forty-fifth largest U.S. cities, Pennsylvania has remained mostly rural, with values and interests to match. The two most popular pastimes in western Pennsylvania, for example, are high school football and deer hunting.

Overall, mountains and rivers dominate the landscape, particularly atop the Appalachian Plateau covering northern and western Pennsylvania. In the southeastern corner of the state, across the Allegheny Mountains, a stretch of the Piedmont underlies the fertile farmland of Pennsylvania Dutch country. Beyond lies Philadelphia, perched on a tiny strip of the Atlantic Coastal Plain. Philadelphia and Erie, the state's two most important ports, give Pennsylvania access to both the Atlantic Ocean (via the Delaware River) and the Great Lakes.

Pennsylvania has more than a million licensed hunters of all ages. When its two-week buck-hunting season begins on the first Monday after Thanksgiving, cities across the state become ghost towns. Schools close and businesses run short of help as up to one third of a town's population heads for the woods.

During the nineteenth century, many Amish and Mennonite farmers settled in Lancaster County. Because they came from Germany (and not Holland), one might wonder why they're called the Pennsylvania Dutch. The reason is that the German word for "German" is *Deutsch,* which looks and sounds like *Dutch.*

Three Rivers
At Pittsburgh, once the nation's busiest inland port, the Allegheny and Monongahela rivers meet to form the Ohio. The Ohio River then flows southwest, joining the Mississippi at Cairo, Illinois.

Interstate Highways

National Parks and Refuges

Public Parks

Places of Interest

0	miles	2
0	kilometers	3.2

MARYLAND

Silver Spring

Bethesda

Chevy Chase

Connecticut Ave.

Rock Creek Park

ROCK CREEK

Georgia Ave.

Massachusetts Ave.

National Zoological Park

Rhode Island Ave.

National Arboretum

The White House

Union Station

Anacostia River Park

Lincoln Memorial

The Mall

U.S. Capitol

Washington Monument

Arlington

ANACOSTIA RIVER

Fort DuPont Park

Arlington National Cemetery

Jefferson Memorial

East Potomac Park

66

VIRGINIA

The Pentagon

395

295

Washington National Airport

Bolling Air Force Base

POTOMAC RIVER

Alexandria

Although nearly half the people who live in D.C. work for Uncle Sam, the federal government isn't the only big industry in town. Tourists, from school groups to international visitors, fill up Washington's hotels and restaurants and provide jobs for ticket takers, museum curators, tour guides, and bus drivers.

DID YOU KNOW?

that nearly one in ten D.C. residents is a lawyer?

←——————— 11.5 miles (18.5 km) ———————→

ABOUT WASHINGTON, D.C.

NICKNAME: __	**POPULATION:** 519,000	**FLOWER:** American Beauty rose
CAPITAL: __	**AREA:** 68 sq. mi.	**TREE:** Scarlet oak
STATEHOOD: __	(176 sq km)	**BIRD:** Wood thrush
MOTTO: Justice for all.	**HIGHEST POINT:** 410 ft. (Tenleytown)	
	LOWEST POINT: 1 ft. (Potomac River)	

Washington, D.C.

Each year, nearly twenty million people visit the District of Columbia. They come to see the White House, the Smithsonian Institution, the Lincoln Memorial, and other popular tourist attractions. Yet when they arrive, they cannot help but find another Washington existing within the nation's capital, a troubled city with high crime rates, potholed streets, and nearly as many welfare recipients as taxpayers.

Until 1974, congressional committees governed the district. Then, in response to public pressure, Congress passed the Home Rule Act establishing a locally elected government. Unfortunately, the mayor and city council were so ineffective—and, in some cases, corrupt—that Congress took back control of most city functions in 1995.

D.C. residents, two thirds of whom are black, have no voting representative in Congress because the district isn't part of any state. (The land was given to the federal government by Maryland in 1791.) However, D.C. residents do benefit greatly from the presence of the federal government, which provides hundreds of thousands of jobs and creates many other business opportunities. The presence of so many foreign embassies and international organizations also makes Washington a remarkably cosmopolitan place to live.

Originally, Washington was just one city within the District of Columbia. Yet today the city fills the entire district, and its metropolitan area extends well beyond into the neighboring suburbs of Maryland and Virginia.

Many American cities suffer from urban problems, such as homelessness, yet in Washington, D.C., these problems are particularly severe. For example, D.C. schools have a dropout rate close to 40 percent, the highest in the nation, and the poverty resembles that of an underdeveloped country.

When it was first surveyed in 1791, the District of Columbia formed a square ten miles (16 km) on each side, including land on both banks of the Potomac. In 1846, however, the federal government gave Virginia back its land, reducing the district's size from one hundred to sixty-eight square miles (259 to 176 sq km).

George Washington had the new federal city built at the head of navigation of the Potomac River—that is, at the point beyond which ships couldn't sail upstream because of rapids and waterfalls.

CANADA

POTOMAC RIVER

West
Virginia
page 60

Virginia
page 58

OHIO RIVER

Kentucky
page 46

CUMBERLAND RIVER

TENNESSEE RIVER

ROANOKE RIVER

North Carolina
page 52

Arkansas
page 40

Tennessee
page 56

ARKANSAS RIVER

MISSISSIPPI RIVER

South
Carolina
page 54

SAVANNAH RIVER

RED RIVER

Alabama
page 38

CHATTAHOOCHEE RIVER

Georgia
page 44

SABINE RIVER

Louisiana
page 48

Mississippi
page 50

Florida
page 42

ATLANTIC OCEAN

THE
BAHAMAS

GULF OF MEXICO

CUBA

For geographical purposes, it sometimes makes sense to divide the southern states into three groups. Virginia, the Carolinas, Georgia, and Florida make up the seaboard states. With the exception of Florida, they all slope down from the Appalachian Mountains through the Piedmont to the Atlantic Coastal Plain. On the other hand, much of Alabama, Mississippi, Louisiana, and Arkansas is bottomland, enriched by the annual flooding of rivers such as the Mississippi. Finally, Tennessee, Kentucky, and West Virginia sit atop the rugged Appalachian highlands.

South

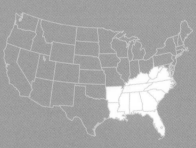

LEGEND

🛣 20 Interstate Highways	⭐ State Capital	▢ Native American Reservations	🌲 National Forests	▲ Highest Point	0 — miles — 50 0 — kilometers — 80

Rocket City, U.S.A.
In 1960, the National Aeronautics and Space Administration (NASA) opened the George C. Marshall Space Flight Center in Huntsville. Since then, many highly trained engineers from around the country have moved to Huntsville to work for the numerous rocketry companies now located there.

DID YOU KNOW?
that half of all U.S. peanuts are grown within one hundred miles (161 km) of Dothan, the self-styled Peanut Capital of the World?

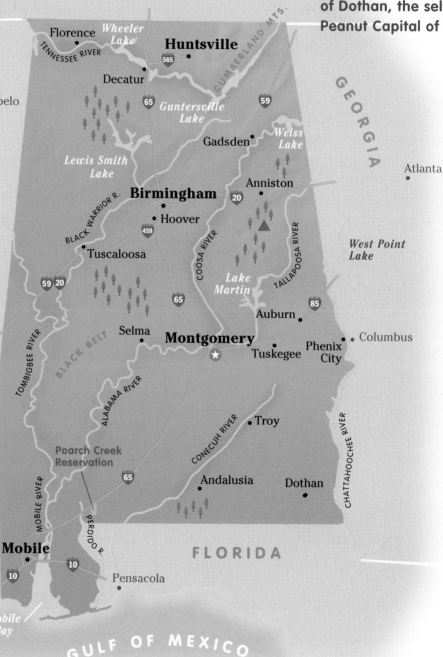

189 miles (304 km)

ABOUT ALABAMA

NICKNAME: Heart of Dixie

CAPITAL: Montgomery

STATEHOOD: December 14, 1819 (22nd)

MOTTO: We dare defend our rights.

POPULATION: 4,369,862 (23rd)

AREA: 52,423 sq. mi. (30th)
(135,717 sq km)

HIGHEST POINT: 2,405 ft. (Cheaha Mountain)

LOWEST POINT: Sea level (Gulf of Mexico)

FLOWER: Camellia

TREE: Southern pine

BIRD: Yellowhammer

FISH: Largemouth bass, tarpon

Alabama

Which changed Alabama more: the Civil War or the boll weevil? Don't answer too quickly. Even after the Civil War, cotton farming continued to dominate the economy, while blacks still suffered from segregation and worse. Then, in 1915, an insect pest called the boll weevil infested Alabama's cotton fields. At the same time, the steel factories in Birmingham began to boom, offering jobs that lured many farm families from the countryside to the city. Together, the boll weevil and the steel jobs urbanized and industrialized what had been a thoroughly rural state.

Today in Alabama, steel, like cotton, has faded in importance, yet new manufacturing industries have taken its place. Paper mills, for example, thrive in Mobile and Montgomery, which makes sense for Alabama because forests cover two thirds of the state. Culturally, though, many Alabamans prefer to live in the past, proudly clinging to traditions commonly associated with the Old South. Some of these are positive, such as the leisurely pace of life, especially during the region's long, hot summers; others reflect problems that still need to be solved, such as the continuing poverty in the countryside.

Although it's difficult to tell from the ground, Alabama is tilted like a washboard. From the state's northeastern corner, where the Appalachian Mountains begin, the land slopes gradually down to the south and west. Following the land, most of Alabama's rivers flow southwest into Mobile Bay.

Traditions are important in Alabama, where most residents can trace their roots back to the nineteenth century. In the black community, which makes up one fourth of the state, churches have been particularly active in social and political causes. Martin Luther King Jr., for example, began his ministerial career at the Dexter Avenue Baptist Church in Montgomery (pictured above).

The key raw materials used in making iron and steel are iron ore, coal, and limestone. Alabama is the only place in the world where these three ingredients can be found within a ten-mile (sixteen-kilometer) radius.

Millions of years ago, the Gulf of Mexico covered southern Alabama. When it receded, it left behind a strip of rich, dark soil called the Black Belt. Once home to grand cotton plantations, the Black Belt now provides pastureland for cattle.

LEGEND

 Interstate Highways

State Capital

National Parks and Refuges

 National Forests

Highest Point

| 0 | miles | 50 |
| 0 | kilometers | 80 |

Even though Arkansas farmers produce nearly half of the nation's rice, the state's most important agricultural product is the broiler chicken. (Broilers are young chickens about seven weeks old.) Arkansas-based Tyson Foods, the world's largest poultry company, processes about forty million birds each week.

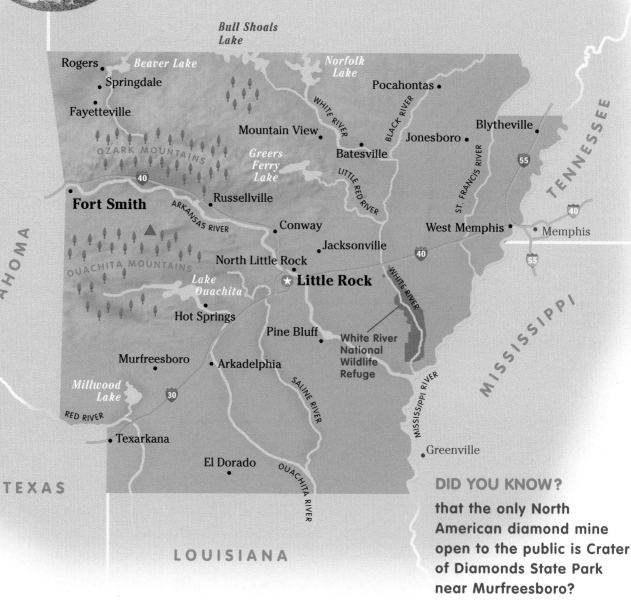

MISSOURI

Bull Shoals Lake

Rogers

Beaver Lake

Norfolk Lake

Springdale

Pocahontas

WHITE RIVER

Fayetteville

Mountain View

BLACK RIVER

Blytheville

Jonesboro

OZARK MOUNTAINS

Greers Ferry Lake

Batesville

ST. FRANCIS RIVER

55

TENNESSEE

Fort Smith

40

Russellville

LITTLE RED RIVER

ARKANSAS RIVER

Conway

West Memphis

Memphis

Jacksonville

40

55

North Little Rock

★ Little Rock

WHITE RIVER

OUACHITA MOUNTAINS

Lake Ouachita

Hot Springs

Pine Bluff

White River National Wildlife Refuge

MISSISSIPPI

Murfreesboro

Arkadelphia

MISSISSIPPI RIVER

Millwood Lake

30

SALINE RIVER

RED RIVER

Texarkana

Greenville

El Dorado

OUACHITA RIVER

OKLAHOMA

TEXAS

LOUISIANA

DID YOU KNOW?

that the only North American diamond mine open to the public is Crater of Diamonds State Park near Murfreesboro?

←———————— 275 miles (442 km) ————————→

ABOUT ARKANSAS

NICKNAME: Land of Opportunity

CAPITAL: Little Rock

STATEHOOD: June 15, 1836 (25th)

MOTTO: The people rule.

POPULATION: 2,551,373 (33rd)

AREA: 53,182 sq. mi. (29th) (137,682 sq km)

HIGHEST POINT: 2,753 ft. (Magazine Mt.)

LOWEST POINT: 55 ft. (Ouachita River)

FLOWER: Apple blossom

TREE: Pine

BIRD: Mockingbird

Arkansas

Little Rock, the state capital, is more than Arkansas's economic and political hub: It's very nearly the wheel itself. Outside this modern city, the rest of the state is mostly countryside, with surprisingly few places to buy a washing machine or a CD. Although tourism has brought many visitors to Arkansas in recent years, the people who live there have changed remarkably little. Nearly 99 percent of them were born in the United States, and more than two thirds were born in Arkansas itself. As a result, the state's population, though racially mixed, isn't culturally diverse.

A diagonal line drawn across Arkansas from the northeast to the southwest would separate the state's lowlands from its highlands. Above this line, which would pass through Little Rock, would be two mountain ranges: the Ouachitas and the Ozarks. The Ouachitas are known for their hot springs, which Native Americans visited for thousands of years before white settlers arrived. The isolated Ozark Plateau features broad ridges and deep valleys cut by fast-moving streams. Separating these ranges is the Arkansas River Valley. Like nearly every river in the state, the Arkansas flows southeast and empties into the Mississippi.

Pine forests cover much of the Arkansas lowlands, yet near the Mississippi River the land has been cleared to allow farming. Once the warm, moist soil produced large harvests of cotton. Now soybeans and rice are the most profitable crops.

During the 1960s, when new roads were built in the Ozarks to encourage tourism, the region became less isolated but also lost some of its individuality. Now the Ozark Folk Center in Mountain View preserves many fading traditions of the mountain people, including their music and crafts such as wood carving and quilt making.

143°F

How Hot Are the Hot Springs?

Two million people a year visit the resort town of Hot Springs on the eastern edge of the Ouachita Mountains. Most go to bathe in the naturally hot mineral water that bubbles from the ground there at 143°F (62°C). According to local Native American tradition, this water is warmed by the breath of the Great Spirit.

The dense pine and hardwood forests that cover the Ozark Plateau once made travel difficult. In this way, the terrain contributed to the isolation of the people who lived there.

41

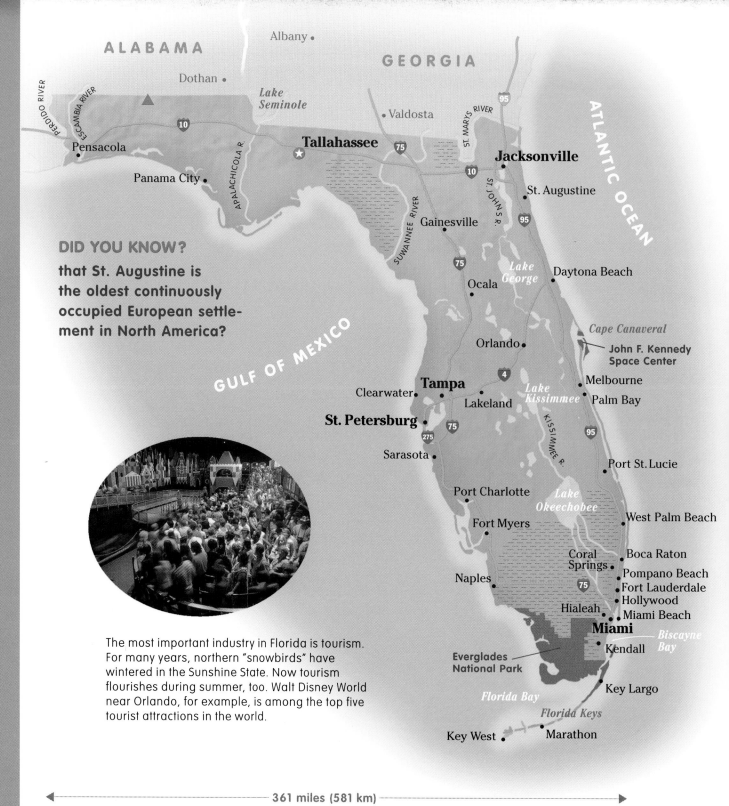

ALABAMA

Albany •

GEORGIA

Dothan •

Lake Seminole

Valdosta •

Tallahassee

Jacksonville

Pensacola

Panama City •

APALACHICOLA R.

PERDIDO RIVER

ESCAMBIA RIVER

St. Augustine

ST. MARY'S RIVER

ST. JOHNS R.

Gainesville •

SUWANNEE RIVER

DID YOU KNOW?
that St. Augustine is the oldest continuously occupied European settlement in North America?

Ocala •

Lake George

Daytona Beach

Cape Canaveral

Orlando •

John F. Kennedy Space Center

GULF OF MEXICO

Tampa

Clearwater •

Lakeland •

Melbourne

Palm Bay

Lake Kissimmee

St. Petersburg •

Sarasota •

KISSIMMEE R.

Port St. Lucie

Port Charlotte •

Lake Okeechobee

West Palm Beach

Fort Myers •

Coral Springs

Boca Raton

Pompano Beach

Fort Lauderdale

Hollywood

Naples •

Hialeah •

Miami Beach

Miami

Biscayne Bay

Kendall

Everglades National Park

Key Largo

Florida Bay

Florida Keys

Key West •

Marathon

The most important industry in Florida is tourism. For many years, northern "snowbirds" have wintered in the Sunshine State. Now tourism flourishes during summer, too. Walt Disney World near Orlando, for example, is among the top five tourist attractions in the world.

◄—————— 361 miles (581 km) ——————►

ABOUT FLORIDA

NICKNAME: Sunshine State	**POPULATION:** 15,111,244 (4th)	**FLOWER:** Orange blossom
CAPITAL: Tallahassee	**AREA:** 65,756 sq. mi. (22nd)	**TREE:** Sabal palm
STATEHOOD: March 3, 1845 (27th)	(170,234 sq km)	**BIRD:** Mockingbird
MOTTO: In God we trust.	**HIGHEST POINT:** 345 ft. (Walton County)	
	LOWEST POINT: Sea level (Atlantic Ocean)	

Florida

The typically warm, sunny weather in Florida affects nearly every aspect of life there. Nearly fifty million tourists a year visit the state to enjoy its tropical climate, and the plentiful sunshine also attracts many retirees. In fact, so many older Americans have moved to Florida, the southernmost of the continental states, that it now has the highest percentage of residents over age sixty-five of any state. Another factor contributing to the diversity of Florida's population is immigration, particularly the arrival of many Cuban and Haitian refugees. Overall, Florida has one of the lowest percentages of residents who were born in the state.

Many of the newcomers, especially the well-to-do retirees, live in condominiums lining the bone-white Gold Coast beaches between Miami and West Palm Beach. The Florida Keys, small limestone-and-coral islands off the state's southern tip, are another chic resort area. Northern Florida, however, is predominantly rural, resembling its neighbors Alabama and Georgia much more than it resembles sophisticated Latin-flavored Miami.

Finally, Florida is the flattest state. Its highest point, in the Panhandle near the Alabama border, is 345 feet (105 m) above sea level. Farther south, on the peninsula separating the Atlantic Ocean from the Gulf of Mexico, the average elevation is less than 100 feet (30 m) above sea level.

Florida's Spanish Accent
In 1513, Spanish explorer Juan Ponce de León became the first European to discover Florida. Since then, Hispanic culture has been an important part of Florida's architecture, cuisine, and lifestyle. Today, most Spanish-speaking Floridians live in and around Miami, where many Cubans have settled.

The orchards of central Florida dominate U.S. citrus production. About 80 percent of the nation's oranges and grapefruit are grown in the state, where nine out of every ten oranges are used to make orange juice.

Florida's most unusual topographical feature, and one of the country's most important wildlife refuges, is the Everglades. Although most people think of the Everglades as a swamp, it's actually a shallow river fifty miles (80 km) wide that carries overflow from Lake Okeechobee into Florida Bay. Its average depth is six inches (15 cm).

🛣 20	⭐	⬛	🌲🌲🌲	〰	🔺	
Interstate Highways	State Capital	National Parks and Refuges	National Forests	Marshlands	Highest Point	0 ___ miles ___ 50 0 ___ kilometers ___ 80

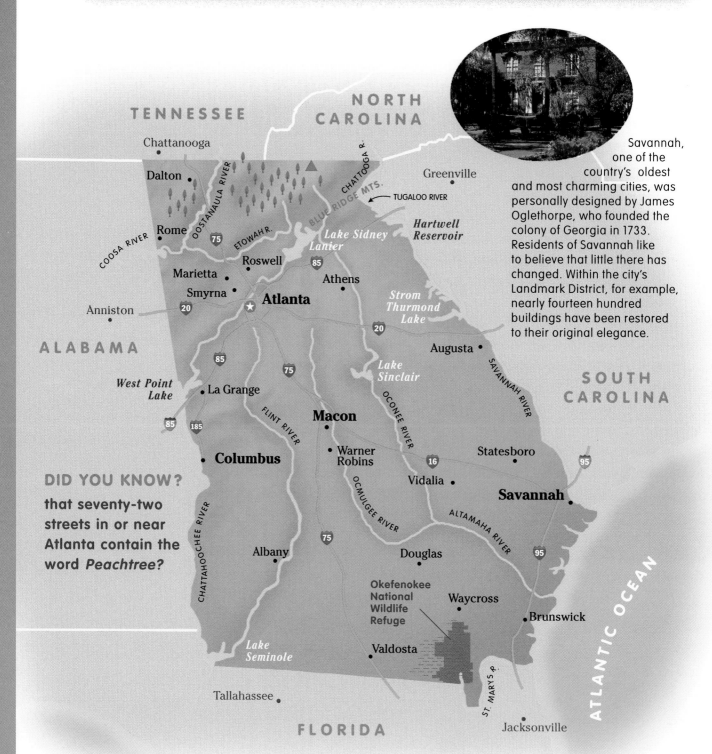

TENNESSEE

NORTH CAROLINA

Chattanooga

Dalton

Greenville

COOSA RIVER

OOSTANAULA RIVER

Rome

ETOWAH R.

CHATTOOGA R.

BLUE RIDGE MTS.

← TUGALOO RIVER

Lake Sidney Lanier

Hartwell Reservoir

Marietta

Roswell

Smyrna

Athens

Anniston

Atlanta

Strom Thurmond Lake

ALABAMA

Augusta

SAVANNAH RIVER

SOUTH CAROLINA

West Point Lake

La Grange

Lake Sinclair

OCONEE RIVER

FLINT RIVER

Macon

DID YOU KNOW?

that seventy-two streets in or near Atlanta contain the word *Peachtree?*

Columbus

Warner Robins

Statesboro

OCMULGEE RIVER

Vidalia

Savannah

ALTAMAHA RIVER

CHATTAHOOCHEE RIVER

Albany

Douglas

ATLANTIC OCEAN

Okefenokee National Wildlife Refuge

Waycross

Brunswick

Lake Seminole

Valdosta

ST. MARY'S R.

Tallahassee

FLORIDA

Jacksonville

Savannah, one of the country's oldest and most charming cities, was personally designed by James Oglethorpe, who founded the colony of Georgia in 1733. Residents of Savannah like to believe that little there has changed. Within the city's Landmark District, for example, nearly fourteen hundred buildings have been restored to their original elegance.

◄---- 254 miles (409 km) ----►

ABOUT GEORGIA

NICKNAME: Empire State of the South

CAPITAL: Atlanta

STATEHOOD: January 2, 1788 (4th)

MOTTO: Wisdom, justice, moderation.

POPULATION: 7,788,240 (10th)

AREA: 59,441 sq. mi. (24th) (153,886 sq km)

HIGHEST POINT: 4,784 ft. (Brasstown Bald)

LOWEST POINT: Sea level (Atlantic Ocean)

FLOWER: Cherokee rose

TREE: Live oak

BIRD: Brown thrasher

FISH: Largemouth bass

Georgia

At one time a cotton state like its neighbors, Georgia now finds itself at the head of the New South, the name given to those states in the region that have successfully updated their economies. The key has been diversification. Cotton now makes up just 2 percent of Georgia's farm income, replaced by peanuts, pecans, and peaches—all crops in which Georgia leads the nation. The state also ranks high in the production of granite, marble, wood pulp, aircraft, textiles, and the fine china clays used to make dinnerware.

Another important step in Georgia's economic revival was the civil rights movement of the 1960s, which pushed the state to become more progressive and cosmopolitan. White Georgians learned to work with, not against, blacks, who make up more than one quarter of the population. Some black Georgians still live on farms, yet many more have moved to the cities, particularly Atlanta, where a strong black middle class has emerged.

In northern Georgia, the Blue Ridge Mountains dot the landscape with "balds," or treeless hilltops. From Atlanta south, however, the belly of the state sits on the rolling Piedmont Plateau, which itself slopes down to the wetlands of the Atlantic and Gulf coastal plains. Along the Florida border is the huge Okefenokee Swamp, one of the nation's leading bird refuges. In the language of the Seminole, *okefenokee* means "land of the trembling earth."

Any item of woven or knit cloth is generally called a textile. Although Georgia trails North Carolina in overall textile production, it leads the nation in carpet making. The center of this industry is the Dalton area, which produces 80 percent of the nation's carpeting.

Atlanta, the acknowledged capital of the New South, has been sucking up Georgians like a vacuum cleaner. At least two out of every five now live within the Atlanta metropolitan area, which has become the most important commercial, financial, and transportation center south of Washington, D.C., and east of Dallas.

Georgia's Piedmont Plateau is known for its red clay hills. "I have a dream," Atlanta native Martin Luther King Jr. said in his famous speech, "that one day on the red hills of Georgia, sons of former slaves and the sons of former slave owners will be able to sit down together at the table of brotherhood."

LEGEND

Interstate Highways	State Capital	National Parks and Refuges	National Forests	Highest Point	0 miles 50 / 0 kilometers 80

Most Kentucky coal is strip-mined by power shovels that tear away the surface layer of trees, rocks, and soil. Because strip mining can pollute streams and destroy animal habitats, Kentuckians often have to choose between a healthy economy and a healthy ecology.

DID YOU KNOW ?

that bluegrass gets its name from the tiny bluish blossoms that the green grass produces each May?

←————————— 350 miles (563 km) —————————→

ABOUT KENTUCKY

NICKNAME: Bluegrass State

CAPITAL: Frankfort

STATEHOOD: June 1, 1792 (15th)

MOTTO: United we stand, divided we fall.

POPULATION: 3,960,825 (25th)

AREA: 40,411 sq. mi. (37th)
(104,619 sq km)

HIGHEST POINT: 4,139 ft. (Black Mountain)

LOWEST POINT: 257 ft. (Mississippi River)

FLOWER: Goldenrod

TREE: Tulip tree

BIRD: Kentucky cardinal

FISH: Bass

Kentucky

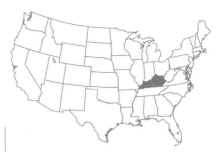

More so than other states, Kentucky is both rich and poor, beautiful and ugly. Its many waterways are among the most scenic in the nation, but elsewhere strip mining for coal has scarred the landscape. Similarly, great wealth exists alongside enduring poverty. In the Cumberland coalfields, labor unions have struggled for decades, sometimes violently, to raise unfairly low wages and improve dangerous working conditions. Yet not too far away, Lexington's immaculate horse farms recall the splendor and gentility of the pre–Civil War South.

Although the Kentucky economy has diversified in recent years—adding automobile plants, for example—it continues to depend on two traditional exports: coal and tobacco. Kentucky ranks second in tobacco behind North Carolina and third in coal behind Wyoming and West Virginia. Other notable Kentucky products are bourbon whiskey and grass seed.

Six major geographical regions cover the state: The coal-rich Cumberland Plateau, part of the Appalachian chain, dominates eastern Kentucky. In the north, surrounding Lexington, are the rolling fields of the Bluegrass. Enclosing the Bluegrass is a horseshoe-shaped line of hills called the Knobs, to the south and west of which lies the flat fertile Pennyroyal. Along the Ohio River are the Western Coal Fields, while in the southwestern corner is the Jackson Purchase, an area bounded by the Mississippi, Tennessee, and Ohio rivers and named after Andrew Jackson, who helped buy it from the Chickasaw in 1818.

Bluegrass, the folk music of this predominantly rural state, resembles old-time string-band music, except that it's faster, higher pitched, and more strident. Bill Monroe, who grew up in Rosine, developed the bluegrass style after World War II. Bluegrass features mandolins, fiddles, and especially banjos.

Beneath the Pennyroyal near Bowling Green is Mammoth Cave, the largest known cave system in the world. Its maze of tunnels and chambers was formed over millions of years by water trickling through limestone bedrock. So far, explorers have charted more than 350 miles (560 km) of tunnels on five underground levels.

The Bluegrass region provides nearly ideal conditions for raising thoroughbred racehorses. The lush grass on which these horses feed absorbs calcium from the limestone bedrock. This calcium promotes strong bones and muscles. The best thoroughbreds compete each May in the Kentucky Derby, run at the Churchill Downs racetrack in Louisville.

LEGEND

 Interstate Highways

State Capital

National Parks and Refuges

National Forests

Marshlands

▲ Highest Point

| 0 | miles | 50 |
| 0 | kilometers | 80 |

Texarkana

ARKANSAS

Caddo Lake

Lake Claiborne

Lake Bayou D'Arbonne

Shreveport

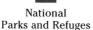 Bossier City

20 Monroe

▲

Vicksburg

OUACHITA RIVER

TENSAS RIVER

RED RIVER

MISSISSIPPI

Toledo Bend Reservoir

Catahoula Lake

Natchez

BLACK R.

Alexandria

TEXAS

De Ridder

MISSISSIPPI RIVER

49

ATCHAFALAYA R.

PEARL RIVER

55

Baton Rouge

10 12

Lake Maurepas

12

SABINE RIVER

Lake Charles

10

Lafayette

10

55

Slidell

59

10

Beaumont

Grand Lake

New Iberia

Six Mile Lake

Lake Pontchartrain

Kenner

New Orleans

Sabine National Wildlife Refuge

Calcasieu Lake

White Lake

Metairie

Houma

MISSISSIPPI RIVER

GULF OF MEXICO

DID YOU KNOW?
that because the early French and Spanish rulers of Louisiana were all Catholics, the state is divided into parishes rather than counties?

Offshore oil and gas exploration was pioneered off the coast of Louisiana. The state is currently the nation's third leading petroleum producer (behind Alaska and Texas) and its second leading producer of natural gas (behind Texas).

◄———————— 237 miles (381 km) ————————►

ABOUT LOUISIANA

NICKNAME: Pelican State
CAPITAL: Baton Rouge
STATEHOOD: April 30, 1812 (18th)
MOTTO: Union, justice, confidence.

POPULATION: 4,372,035 (22nd)
AREA: 51,843 sq. mi. (31st)
(134,215 sq km)
HIGHEST POINT: 535 ft. (Driskill Mountain)
LOWEST POINT: -8 ft. (New Orleans)

FLOWER: Magnolia
TREE: Bald cypress
BIRD: Brown pelican

Louisiana

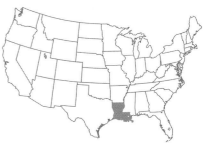

Before the United States purchased Louisiana in 1803, it had been both a French and a Spanish colony. There were also slaves in the territory, brought to work on the numerous cotton plantations. Over time, these three cultures merged to form what's today known as Creole.

The Cajuns, who live in Louisiana's southern bayous, also have French roots, yet theirs came by way of Canada. In 1755, the British expelled about ten thousand French colonists from Acadia (now Nova Scotia), and many made their way south to Louisiana. Lately, the national popularity of zydeco music has stimulated a resurgence of the Cajun French language and culture.

Blacks, who make up 32 percent of the population, were long denied economic and political power in Louisiana. Yet they made important cultural contributions. Jazz music, for example, was invented by black performers in New Orleans about 1900.

Although agriculture remains important in Louisiana, the state's economy now depends more on shipping, petroleum, and the chemical industry. Between Baton Rouge and New Orleans, the banks of the Mississippi River are lined with chemical plants and oil refineries. In general, the Mississippi dominates the physical geography of the state. The southern half is remarkably flat, with low-lying swamps and a beachless coastline. As one moves north, however, the land rises slowly to prairies and low hills.

Nothing shows off Louisiana's rich cultural mix so much as its cooking. The world-famous Creole cuisine of New Orleans is a distinctive yet elegant blend of French, Spanish, and African dishes. In bayou country, however, Cajuns favor much spicier food, such as gumbo (a stew) and jambalaya (a rice dish).

Rivers are constantly depositing sediment along their banks as well as on their bottoms. Sometimes this sediment builds up so high the river rises to a level above that of the surrounding land. This has happened at New Orleans, where levees have been constructed to protect the city from flooding.

A bayou is a stream that moves slowly through marshland. The bayous of southern Louisiana provide important habitats for migrating birds, especially the wild ducks and geese that winter there.

LEGEND

🛣 20	⭐	◻	🌲	◼	▲	0 — miles — 50
Interstate Highways	State Capital	Native American Reservations	National Forests	National Parks and Refuges	Highest Point	0 — kilometers — 80

TENNESSEE

Memphis

Pickwick Lake

Southaven · Holly Springs

ARKANSAS

Sardis Lake

Clarksdale

Oxford

TENNESSEE HILLS ▲

Tupelo

55

YALOBUSHA R.

Cleveland

Grenada Lake

Greenwood

Columbus

TOMBIGBEE RIVER

Starkville

Greenville

TALLAHATCHIE R.

YAZOO RIVER

BLACK PRAIRIE

Yazoo City

BIG BLACK RIVER

Mississippi Choctaw Reservation

ALABAMA

Ross Barnett Reservoir

20

Vicksburg

★ **Jackson**

20 59

Meridian

LOUISIANA

MISSISSIPPI RIVER

PEARL RIVER

Laurel

Natchez

55

Hattiesburg

59

Mississippi Sandhill Crane National Wildlife Refuge

Mobile

Baton Rouge

Gulfport

10

Biloxi · Pascagoula

New Orleans

GULF OF MEXICO

In Mississippi, many farmers have turned unproductive cotton fields into profitable catfish farms by flooding them. These aquaculturists fatten young catfish on grain before harvesting them, just as any farmer would fatten a cow or chicken before sending it to the slaughterhouse.

DID YOU KNOW?

that Mississippi Delta topsoil is as deep as twenty-five feet (8 m) in some places?

← — 188 miles (302 km) — →

ABOUT MISSISSIPPI

NICKNAME: Magnolia State
CAPITAL: Jackson
STATEHOOD: December 10, 1817 (20th)
MOTTO: By valor and arms.

POPULATION: 2,768,619 (31st)
AREA: 48,434 sq. mi. (32nd)
(125,390 sq km)
HIGHEST POINT: 806 ft. (Woodall Mountain)
LOWEST POINT: Sea level (Gulf of Mexico)

FLOWER: Magnolia
TREE: Magnolia
BIRD: Mockingbird
FISH: Largemouth bass

Mississippi

Of all the states, Mississippi has long been the poorest, placing last year after year in nearly every economic ranking. Ineffective schools and depleted soil were part of the problem, but at its core was the inequality that existed between whites and blacks. (Blacks make up 36 percent of the population, the highest percentage of any state.) As late as the 1960s, blacks were commonly denied the right to vote and the opportunity to earn a decent living. Only since the civil rights movement has a majority of white Mississippians realized that keeping blacks down meant keeping the state down as well. Now that black and white Mississippians are finally working together, economic conditions have at last begun to improve.

Agriculture remains fundamental to the economy of this mainly rural state, yet manufacturing has become an increasingly vital part of the mix. In recent years, for example, many Mississippians have moved south to work in the shipyards at Pascagoula or for one of the oil and gas companies lining the Gulf Coast.

Although not as important economically as it once was, the Mississippi River remains the most important geographic feature in the state's flat landscape. The river's floodplain, a region known as the Delta, is quite narrow south of Vicksburg. In northern Mississippi, however, it widens to include the entire basin between the Mississippi and Yazoo rivers.

Faulkner Country
Mississippi has produced many great writers, including Eudora Welty, Tennessee Williams, and especially William Faulkner. Setting his books in small-town Mississippi, Faulkner made fictional Yoknapatawpha County one of the most celebrated locations in American literature. For the last thirty years of his life, Faulkner lived at Rowan Oak in Oxford (pictured above).

Most naturally occurring lakes in Mississippi are oxbows, formed by sudden changes in the course of the Mississippi River. Although the center of the river marks the state's boundary with Louisiana and Arkansas, land cut off from Mississippi by abrupt course changes still belongs to Mississippi.

The topsoil of the Mississippi Delta is particularly rich because for thousands of years annual flooding dumped tons and tons of silt over the land. Now artificial levees of earth, sand, rock, and concrete keep the river generally within its banks.

LEGEND

20 Interstate Highways	★ State Capital	Native American Reservations	National Forests	National Parks and Refuges	Marshlands	▲ Highest Point	0 miles 50 / 0 km 80

North Carolina leads the nation in the production of both tobacco and tobacco products, such as cigarettes. Tobacco fields blanket much of the Piedmont, where farmers have been reluctant to give up their way of life even though tobacco has been shown to be a health hazard.

VIRGINIA

Buggs Island Lake

Virginia Beach

Great Smoky Mountains National Park

TENN.

YADKIN RIVER

BLUE RIDGE MOUNTAINS

77

Greensboro Burlington

Lake Gaston

CHOWAN R.

ROANOKE R.

85

Knoxville

Winston-Salem

CATAWBA R.

High Point

Chapel Hill

Durham

95

Raleigh ★ Rocky Mount

40

Cary

Wilson

Asheville

40

Lake Norman

85

UHARIE R.

Greenville

26

Lake Tillery

Goldsboro

Gastonia

Charlotte

NEUSE RIVER

Cape Hatteras

85

Fayetteville

40

PEE DEE RIVER

77

95

Jacksonville

SOUTH CAROLINA

CAPE FEAR RIVER

Cape Lookout

Wilmington

GEORGIA

Columbia

Cape Fear

ATLANTIC OCEAN

DID YOU KNOW?

that North Carolina's Mount Mitchell is the highest point east of the Mississippi River?

◄────────── 503 miles (809 km) ──────────►

ABOUT NORTH CAROLINA

NICKNAME: Tar Heel State

CAPITAL: Raleigh

STATEHOOD: November 21, 1789 (12th)

MOTTO: To be rather than to seem.

POPULATION: 7,650,789 (11th)

AREA: 53,821 sq. mi. (28th) (139,336 sq km)

HIGHEST POINT: 6,684 ft. (Mount Mitchell)

LOWEST POINT: Sea level (Atlantic Ocean)

FLOWER: Flowering dogwood

TREE: Longleaf pine

BIRD: Cardinal

FISH: Channel bass

North Carolina

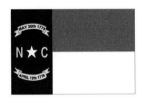

Most of North Carolina's major rivers begin along the state's western edge, where the Blue Ridge and Great Smoky mountains rise up to form the highest peaks in the long Appalachian chain. From these mountains, where the people practice handicrafts much as their ancestors did, the water flows east in narrow, swift-moving streams down to the Piedmont Plateau. That's where North Carolina's largest cities are located and where most of its money is made. On the busy Piedmont, furniture and textile manufacturers add considerably to the even larger profits of the tobacco industry.

Passing into the Tidewater region, North Carolina's rivers slow and widen as they spread across the Atlantic Coastal Plain. The pace of life in this rural area slows considerably as well. Extending about one hundred miles (161 km) inland, the Tidewater covers a great deal of marshland as well as the southern end of the Great Dismal Swamp. Because of their shallow estuaries, North Carolina's rivers don't make useful points of entry for shipping. However, the abundance of shrimp, blue crab, and flounder in the state's coastal waters makes them excellent for commercial fishing.

Overall, North Carolina ranks among the top ten states in industrial jobs. Yet wages remain low because so many of those jobs, especially in the tobacco industry, require little skill or training.

The eleven thousand Cherokee in North Carolina make up one of the largest Native American populations east of the Mississippi River. Their reservation is located at the base of the Great Smoky Mountains, where their ancestors fled during the late 1830s to escape forced removal by the government.

0	20 km
0	15 mi

City Limits

Since 1959, local business leaders have been working with the three Triangle universities—Duke (in Durham), North Carolina State (in Raleigh), and the University of North Carolina at Chapel Hill—to create a world-class research facility. The result, Research Triangle Park, specializes in such high-tech fields as supercomputing and biotechnology.

The long, thin islands that fringe much of North Carolina's coast are called the Outer Banks. These enormous sandbars protect the mainland from high winds and erosion caused by the pounding Atlantic surf.

LEGEND

20 Interstate Highways	✪ State Capital	■ National Parks and Refuges	National Forests	Marshlands	▲ Highest Point	0 — miles — 50 0 — kilometers — 80

DID YOU KNOW?
that South Carolina's coastal swamps are home to most poisonous snakes found in the United States?

NORTH CAROLINA

Charlotte

BLUE RIDGE MOUNTAINS

CHATTOOGA R.
TUGALOO R.
SENECA R.
Lake Keowee
Hartwell Reservoir

26
85
Spartanburg
Greenville
385
85
Anderson
SALUDA RIVER
26

Wylie Lake
Rock Hill
CATAWBA RIVER
77
BROAD RIVER

Cheraw

Wateree Lake

95

Greenwood

Strom Thurmond Lake

Lake Murray
Columbia ✪
CONGAREE R.

WATEREE R.

20
Sumter
20
95

Florence
Lake City

Myrtle Beach

PEE DEE RIVER

Georgetown

20
Augusta

GEORGIA

SAVANNAH RIVER

Congaree Swamp National Monument
Orangeburg
26

Lake Marion

Lake Moultrie
26

SANTEE RIVER
COOPER R.

Walterboro

95
Beaufort

Charleston

Kiawah Island

ATLANTIC OCEAN

Savannah
Hilton Head Island

A textile is an item made from woven or knitted cloth. In South Carolina's Textile Belt, which runs through Spartanburg and Greenville, owners of textile factories benefit from a relatively low cost of labor.

◄------------ 273 miles (439 km) ------------►

ABOUT SOUTH CAROLINA

NICKNAME: Palmetto State
CAPITAL: Columbia
STATEHOOD: May 23, 1788 (8th)
MOTTO: While I breathe, I hope.

POPULATION: 3,885,736 (26th)
AREA: 32,008 sq. mi. (40th)
(82,865 sq km)
HIGHEST POINT: 3,560 ft. (Sassafras Mt.)
LOWEST POINT: Sea level (Atlantic Ocean)

FLOWER: Yellow jessamine
TREE: Palmetto
BIRD: Carolina wren
FISH: Striped bass

South Carolina

South Carolina, like its neighbors, was once an agricultural state dependent on cotton and slave labor. Since the Civil War, however, tobacco and greenhouse crops have overtaken cotton as the most important crops, just as other sectors of the economy have overtaken agriculture. Yet South Carolina retains much of its pre–Civil War cultural heritage. For example, the state's tradition of soldiering has been preserved at both The Citadel in Charleston, one of the nation's premier military colleges, and the renowned Marine Corps training center on Parris Island, near Beaufort.

When it comes to geography, the people of South Carolina like to keep things simple: They call the flat land near the coast the Low Country and everything else the Up Country. Covering about two thirds of the state, the Low Country—what geographers call the Atlantic Coastal Plain—features many slow-moving rivers that feed swamps and marshes near the coast.

The Up Country—or, more formally, the Piedmont Plateau—begins just west of Columbia, the state capital. Rising gradually from east to west, the Piedmont ends at the Blue Ridge Mountains, which cut across the northwestern corner of the state. Columbia itself sits atop a line of sandy hills marking the point at which the South Carolina shoreline once stood millions of years ago.

Many black descendants of slaves live on the Sea Islands, extending south into Georgia and Florida. Isolation has helped preserve their unique language, Gullah, which mixes seventeenth-century English with several African languages. *Goober* (meaning "peanut") and *hoodoo* (meaning "bad luck") were both originally Gullah words.

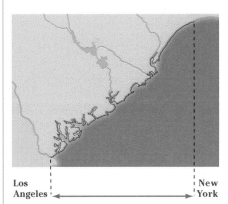

Los Angeles — New York

It's a Stretch
As the crow flies, South Carolina's coastline is 187 miles (301 km) long. However, because there are so many inlets and islands south of Georgetown, the coastline that you would walk is actually much longer. If you could pull it straight, it would be about 3,000 miles (about 5,000 km) long.

From Pawleys Island (near Georgetown) to the North Carolina border stretches a sixty-mile (hundred-kilometer) crescent of white-sand beach called the Grand Strand. First among Grand Strand resorts is Myrtle Beach, a top-ten U.S. tourist destination.

LEGEND

〰20〰	✪	■	♣♣♣	▲	0 miles 50	
Interstate Highways	State Capital	National Parks and Refuges	National Forests	Highest Point	0 kilometers 80	

During World War II, the War Department built in a hidden Cumberland Mountain valley a top-secret town for scientists working on the atom bomb. Today, researchers at the Oak Ridge National Laboratory conduct all sorts of experiments, such as this one to help detect airborne pollutants.

An aerial view of Oak Ridge National Laboratory.

DID YOU KNOW?

that Tennessee's only large natural lake, Reelfoot, was created when violent earthquakes in 1811 and 1812 formed a depression into which water from the Mississippi River flowed?

430 miles (692 km)

ABOUT TENNESSEE

NICKNAME: Volunteer State

CAPITAL: Nashville

STATEHOOD: June 1, 1796 (16th)

MOTTO: Agriculture and commerce.

POPULATION: 5,483,535 (16th)

AREA: 42,146 sq. mi. (36th)
(109,111 sq km)

HIGHEST POINT: 6,643 ft. (Clingmans Dome)

LOWEST POINT: 178 ft. (Mississippi River)

FLOWER: Iris

TREE: Tulip tree

BIRD: Mockingbird

Tennessee

Tennessee has always been a divided state. During the Civil War, for example, the mountain people of eastern Tennessee remained loyal to the Union while the residents of middle and western Tennessee seceded to join the Confederacy. As a result, more Civil War battles were fought in Tennessee than in any other state except Virginia.

In many ways, Tennessee remains a divided state, caught between North and South. Its culture, especially in western Tennessee, is profoundly southern in style and taste. Clear distinctions are made between social classes (as between races), and the wealthiest residents lead uncommonly gracious lives. Tennessee's economy, however, is much more northern in character. Because 70 percent of the state is considered unfit for cultivation, Tennessee has industrialized more rapidly than its neighbors. Until recently, the chemical industry was ranked first in the state, but now, with new automobile factories in Spring Hill (Saturn) and Smyrna (Nissan), transportation equipment tops the list of its products.

Rugged eastern Tennessee takes in both the Great Smoky Mountains and the high, hilly Cumberland Plateau. West of the Cumberland Mountains sits the Nashville Basin, the most prominent geographical feature of middle Tennessee, which ends at the Tennessee River. The flatlands on the other side of that river make up western Tennessee—whose principal city, Memphis, is the second largest inland port on the Mississippi.

Nashville, the Tennessee state capital, is probably better known as the Country Music Capital of the World. Ever since radio station WSM began broadcasting live performances from the Grand Ole Opry in 1925, songwriters and performers have flocked to Nashville's Music Row to make it in the music business.

) dams

A Powerful River

In 1933, Congress created the Tennessee Valley Authority (TVA). Its mission was to build dams along the Tennessee River that would control flooding, improve navigation, and generate electricity. The TVA currently operates twenty-nine dams producing cheap hydroelectric power.

The Great Smoky Mountains of eastern Tennessee get their name from the bluish haze that usually covers them. This "smoke" is actually a mixture of water vapor and evaporated plant oils.

The hub of the navy's Atlantic fleet is Hampton Roads, the deepwater channel through which the James River flows into Chesapeake Bay. Norfolk, site of the world's largest naval base, serves as home port to 120 ships, while Newport News Shipbuilding, the largest privately owned U.S. shipyard, builds everything from tugboats to nuclear-powered aircraft carriers.

DID YOU KNOW?

that the Pentagon in Arlington, with 23,000 workers and 284 rest rooms, is one of the world's largest office buildings?

← 440 miles (708 km) →

ABOUT VIRGINIA

NICKNAME: Old Dominion	**POPULATION:** 6,872,912 (12th)	**FLOWER:** Flowering dogwood
CAPITAL: Richmond	**AREA:** 42,777 sq. mi. (35th)	**TREE:** Flowering dogwood
STATEHOOD: June 25, 1788 (10th)	(110,745 sq km)	**BIRD:** Cardinal
MOTTO: Thus always to tyrants.	**HIGHEST POINT:** 5,729 ft. (Mount Rogers)	
	LOWEST POINT: Sea level (Atlantic Ocean)	

Virginia

In George Washington's time, Virginia was a rich agricultural state. Today, however, farming is primarily confined to small family operations. The biggest employer now is the federal government, which accounts for nearly one fifth of the state's total income. The Hampton Roads naval base alone generates some seven billion dollars a year.

The people who live in Virginia's northern counties, many of whom commute to jobs in Washington, D.C., reflect the cosmopolitan makeup of the nation's capital. On the other hand, Richmond still clings to a recognizably southern way of life. In this way, the former Confederate stronghold now forms a convenient bridge between North and South.

Like other southern seaboard states, Virginia slopes down from mountains in the west to marshland in the east. The most important ranges in Virginia, the Blue Ridge and Allegheny mountains, belong to the Appalachian chain. Below them lie the rolling hills of the Piedmont, which gradually descend to the fall line. Here the land "falls" abruptly to the Atlantic Coastal Plain, creating river rapids and waterfalls. (Many Virginia cities—including Alexandria, Fredericksburg, Richmond, and Petersburg—grew up along the fall line to take advantage of its cheap waterpower.) Finally, the low sandy plain surrounding Chesapeake Bay is called the Tidewater because of the effect that the ocean tides have on its inlets and waterways.

Virginia boasts an unusually large number of historic sites, from the homes of George Washington and Thomas Jefferson to important Revolutionary and Civil War battlefields. Among the most popular sites is Colonial Williamsburg, a restoration designed to show visitors the colonial capital as Washington and Jefferson knew it.

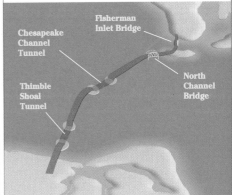

The twenty-three-mile-long (thirty-seven-kilometer-long) Chesapeake Bay Bridge-Tunnel connects the southern side of Hampton Roads with Virginia's Eastern Shore. The structure, the longest of its kind in the world, includes two bridges, four artificial islands, and a pair of tunnels that pass under the bay's two main shipping channels.

The scenic, fertile Shenandoah Valley lies between the Blue Ridge and Allegheny mountains. Its name, of Native American origin, means "daughter of the stars."

Interstate Highways

State Capital

National Parks and Refuges

National Forests

Highest Point

| 0 | miles | 50 |
| 0 | kilometers | 80 |

DID YOU KNOW?

that in West Virginia's thin northern panhandle the city of Weirton stretches across the entire state?

Pittsburgh

PENNSYLVANIA

Weirton

Wheeling

70

OHIO

OHIO RIVER

79

Morgantown

68

Fairmont

Clarksburg

MD.

Cumberland

Hagerstown

Harpers Ferry National Historical Park

NORTH BRANCH POTOMAC R.

Keyser

POTOMAC R.

Martinsburg

Parkersburg

Buckhannon

Elkins

SOUTH BRANCH POTOMAC R.

81

SHENANDOAH R.

77

KANAWHA R.

79

Sutton Lake

ALLEGHENY MOUNTAINS

VIRGINIA

OHIO RIVER

Charleston

64

ELK RIVER

Spruce Knob Seneca Rocks National Reservation Area

Charlottesville

BIG SANDY RIVER

Huntington

South Charleston

GAULEY RIVER

GUYANDOTTE RIVER

77

64

Oak Hill

Beckley

64

KENTUCKY

TUG FORK RIVER

NEW RIVER

77

Bluefield

Roanoke

Since the nineteenth century, the health of West Virginia's economy has depended on coal mining. The huge seams of soft bituminous coal that underlie the state have made it the nation's second largest coal producer (behind Wyoming). Yet this dependence has also bound generations of West Virginians to hard, dangerous work in the mines.

265 miles (426 km)

ABOUT WEST VIRGINIA

NICKNAME: Mountain State
CAPITAL: Charleston
STATEHOOD: June 20, 1863 (35th)
MOTTO: Mountaineers are always free.

POPULATION: 1,806,928 (36th)
AREA: 24,231 sq. mi. (41st) (62,731 sq km)
HIGHEST POINT: 4,861 ft. (Spruce Knob)
LOWEST POINT: 240 ft. (Potomac River)

FLOWER: Rhododendron
TREE: Sugar maple
BIRD: Cardinal
FISH: Brook trout

West Virginia

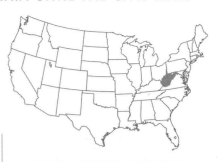

Few states are as rugged as West Virginia. Except for a handful of floodplains surrounding its major rivers, there's almost no level ground. This makes farming difficult and frustrates all sorts of economic development because moving things around is so hard. As a result, West Virginia has remained a state of generally poor, small communities tucked away in steep, narrow hollows. Only one in every three West Virginians lives in a city.

On the other hand, the mountains do supply West Virginia with the mineral wealth that is its main source of income. In addition to coal, West Virginians mine silica-rich sandstone for glassware (and most U.S. marbles), clay for pottery, and salt for dyes, paints, and plastics. The Native American word *kanawha*, meaning "place of the white stone," refers to the large deposits of salt in the Kanawha and Ohio river valleys.

Passing approximately through Elkins, the Allegheny Front separates the Allegheny Plateau, which covers the western two thirds of the state, from the Appalachian Ridge and Valley system in the east. Millions of years ago, the Allegheny Plateau was a high flatland, but over time rivers have eroded the softer rock, creating the present maze of hills and valleys.

Like most natives of Appalachia, West Virginians take great pride in their folk culture, especially the "mountain music" they play on fiddles, dulcimers, mandolins, and other homemade string instruments. Nationally syndicated *Mountain Stage,* produced by West Virginia Public Radio, features this music along with contemporary folk, blues, and even rock 'n' roll.

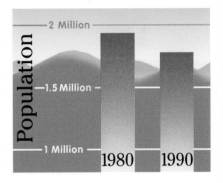

During the 1980s, West Virginia lost more population than any other state, falling from 1,950,186 residents in 1980 to 1,793,477 in 1990. Most of those who left were young people from rural areas who were having trouble finding jobs. Since 1992, the population has stabilized at about 1,800,000.

All of West Virginia lies within the Appalachian Mountains. The state's highest point is Spruce Knob, from whose summit this view was taken.

CANADA

LAKE SUPERIOR

LAKE HURON

LAKE MICHIGAN

LAKE ERIE

Minnesota
page 72

Wisconsin
page 78

Michigan
page 70

Iowa
page 68

MISSOURI RIVER

ILLINOIS RIVER

WABASH RIVER

Ohio
page 76

Illinois
page 64

Indiana
page 66

OHIO RIVER

Missouri
page 74

MISSISSIPPI RIVER

Midwest

During the last Ice Age, huge glaciers covered nearly all the Midwest. Like unfrozen water, these glaciers also flowed, if very slowly. Their movement had the same effect as a giant bulldozer, flattening the land and leaving behind a thick layer of mixed clay and stone, called till. Most of this region now belongs to what geographers call the Dissected Till Plains. (*Dissected* means "cut up," referring in this case to the way that rivers and streams have cut up the tableland.)

Interstate Highways

State Capital

National Forests

Highest Point

| 0 | miles | 50 |
| 0 | kilometers | 80 |

DID YOU KNOW?

that a canal was constructed in 1900 to make the Chicago River flow backward, away from Lake Michigan?

WISCONSIN

LAKE MICHIGAN

Dubuque

Rockford

Kenosha
Waukegan
Elgin
Evanston
DeKalb
Oak Park
Chicago
Aurora
Joliet
Gary

IOWA

Davenport
Moline
Rock Island

Galesburg

Peoria

Kankakee

MISSISSIPPI RIVER

ILLINOIS RIVER

Bloomington

SANGAMON R.

Champaign
Danville
Urbana

INDIANA

Quincy

Decatur

Springfield

Lake Shelbyville

Charleston

Terre Haute

MISSOURI

KASKASKIA R.

Alton

Carlyle Lake

St. Louis
East St. Louis

WABASH RIVER

Rend Lake

Evansville

Carbondale

OHIO RIVER

KENTUCKY

Cairo

Whether you want to ship by land, air, or water, Illinois has the world's greatest concentration of transportation resources. These include Chicago, the most important rail and trucking center in the United States; O'Hare International, the world's busiest airport; and the Great Lakes as well as the Mississippi River.

211 miles (339 km)

ABOUT ILLINOIS

NICKNAME: Prairie State

CAPITAL: Springfield

STATEHOOD: December 3, 1818 (21st)

MOTTO: State sovereignty—national union.

POPULATION: 12,128,370 (5th)

AREA: 57,918 sq. mi. (25th) (149,943 sq km)

HIGHEST POINT: 1,235 ft. (Charles Mound)

LOWEST POINT: 279 ft. (Mississippi River)

FLOWER: Native violet

TREE: White oak

BIRD: Cardinal

FISH: Bluegill

Illinois

If you live in Illinois, you're either a Chicagoan or a downstater. Being a Chicagoan means that you live in the nation's third largest city or one of its many suburbs. Everyone else is a downstater. Maps show that Chicago and the rest of Illinois are connected, yet most Chicagoans don't seem to acknowledge this. Committed city dwellers, they seem to believe that Chicago's immediate neighbors are New York City and Los Angeles, so they rarely think about downstate at all. Downstaters, on the other hand, can hardly ignore Chicago or its sizable impact on state politics. At last count, Chicagoans significantly outnumbered downstaters, and the gap is growing.

Chicago has benefited greatly from its central location and easy access to both the Great Lakes and the Mississippi River. Because the city is a major transportation hub, it can easily import raw materials and ship out finished goods. This has helped it become a major U.S. manufacturing center, second only to the Los Angeles area.

Unlike industrial Chicago, downstate Illinois is rural and agricultural. Primarily flat, with hilly areas only in the northwest and south, it lies almost entirely within the Dissected Till Plains, whose flat topography and rich glacial soil present ideal conditions for farming. As elsewhere in the midwestern farm belt, the major crops in Illinois are corn and soybeans.

Who Governs?
Chicago has attracted many immigrant groups over the years, yet the city has never been a melting pot. Racial and ethnic tensions continue to play important roles in local politics. For example, although Chicago is 40 percent black, the city has had only one black mayor, Harold Washington, who governed from 1983 until his death in 1987.

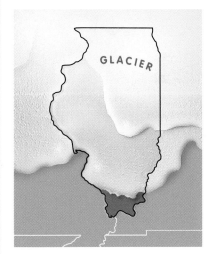

During the last Ice Age, glaciers covered nearly all of Illinois. These huge masses of ice flattened the state, grinding down hills and leaving behind a layer of mineral-rich soil. In other words, they turned Illinois into excellent farmland.

The skyscraper, first developed in Chicago, continues to dominate that city's skyline. Until the 1997 completion of the 1,483-foot (452-meter) Petronas Towers in Malaysia, the 1,450-foot (442-meter) Sears Tower was the world's tallest building.

LEGEND

Interstate Highways   State Capital   National Parks and Refuges   National Forests   Highest Point

0   miles   50
0   kilometers   80

LAKE MICHIGAN

MICHIGAN

Chicago

Michigan City

Hammond   **Gary**   **South Bend**   Elkhart

Goshen

Valparaiso

KANKAKEE RIVER   TIPPECANOE RIVER

MAUMEE R.

Fort Wayne

LITTLE WABASH R.

ST. MARYS R.

Wabash

WABASH R.

Mississinewa Lake   *Salamonie Lake*

Marion

OHIO

Lafayette   Kokomo

Muncie

Anderson

Noblesville

Indianapolis

Richmond

Brookville Lake

Terre Haute

WHITE RIVER

Columbus

Cincinnati

Bloomington

Monroe Lake

EAST FORK WHITE RIVER

Muscatatuck National Wildlife Refuge

ILLINOIS

Vincennes

Washington

Patoka Lake

New Albany   Jeffersonville

Louisville

WABASH R.

Evansville

OHIO RIVER

KENTUCKY

The industrial sprawl around Gary leads the nation in steel production. Yet in exchange for steel's high-paying jobs—jobs that have attracted many southern blacks—residents of Gary must tolerate air pollution that sometimes darkens the sky on sunny days.

DID YOU KNOW?

that *Hoosier,* the nickname for an Indianan, may have come from *hoozer,* an Old English word meaning "anything unusually large," such as the hills of southern Indiana?

◄────── 160 miles (257 km) ──────►

ABOUT INDIANA

NICKNAME: Hoosier State

CAPITAL: Indianapolis

STATEHOOD: December 11, 1816 (19th)

MOTTO: The crossroads of America.

POPULATION: 5,942,901 (14th)

AREA: 36,420 sq. mi. (38th)
(94,287 sq km)

HIGHEST POINT: 1,257 ft. (Franklin Township)

LOWEST POINT: 320 ft. (Ohio River)

FLOWER: Peony

TREE: Tulip tree

BIRD: Cardinal

Indiana

The landscape of Indiana, like that of Illinois and Iowa, was shaped by the glaciers that covered the Midwest during the last Ice Age. In the northern third of the state, these glaciers left behind many hollows that became kettle lakes. In central Indiana, they flattened the land and deposited a rocky debris called till. Over time, the sand, clay, and minerals that made up the till eroded into a thick layer of highly fertile soil. Only the southern sixth of Indiana, a region rich in coal and limestone, escaped the glaciers, and so only its hills were preserved.

Farms established on Indiana's central flatlands flourished during the nineteenth century. Since 1900, however, manufacturing has become increasingly important to the state, particularly in its northwestern corner, which abuts Lake Michigan. Gary, for example, became a popular location for steel plants because it lay halfway between the iron ranges of Minnesota and the coalfields of southern Indiana.

The population of Indiana is only 8 percent black. Yet the city of Gary is 81 percent black because nearly all the blacks in Indiana live there—or in Fort Wayne or Indianapolis. The rest of the state, except for a large Polish community in South Bend, is typically white, Protestant, and English, Irish, or German in descent.

No sport arouses the passion of Hoosiers the way that basketball does. That's why the state's annual high school basketball tournament is called Hoosier Hysteria. It may be that basketball, a winter sport, is so popular in Indiana, a farming state, because it has never had to compete with spring planting or the fall harvest season.

Then   Now

Where Have All the Forests Gone?
When white settlers first came to Indiana during the early nineteenth century, 80 percent of the state was covered with trees, especially beeches, oaks, sycamores, and maples. Then these pioneers began clearing the land for farms. Today, only 17 percent of Indiana remains forested.

Indiana limestone has been used to face the Empire State Building, the Pentagon, and many other celebrated structures. Workers in the quarries around Bloomington, which produce the finest limestone, are called cutters.

LEGEND

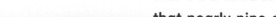

Interstate Highways	State Capital	National Parks and Refuges	Highest Point	0 — miles — 50 / 0 — kilometers — 80

DID YOU KNOW?

that nearly nine out of ten Iowans graduate from high school (compared to seven out of ten nationwide)?

MINNESOTA

Sioux Falls

S.D.

BIG SIOUX RIVER

Spencer

Mason City

Effigy Mounds National Monument

WISCONSIN

CEDAR RIVER

LITTLE SIOUX RIVER

Sioux City

Storm Lake

Fort Dodge

Cedar Falls
Waterloo

Dubuque

MISSISSIPPI RIVER

MISSOURI RIVER

Ames

Marshalltown

Cedar Rapids

Clinton

IOWA RIVER

Urbandale

Des Moines

Iowa City

Davenport

Red Rock Lake

Muscatine

Rock Island

Omaha

Council Bluffs

Indianola

Ottumwa

DES MOINES RIVER

Burlington

NEBRASKA

Rathbun Lake

ILLINOIS

MISSOURI

Most Iowans work in jobs related to farming. Although just 4 percent actually farm the land, many more have jobs in food-processing plants or factories making farm equipment. Waterloo has meat-packing and tractor plants, Cedar Rapids and Keokuk have large cereal mills, and Sioux City has the world's largest popcorn factory (pictured here).

◄——————— 324 miles (521 km) ———————►

ABOUT IOWA

NICKNAME: Hawkeye State

CAPITAL: Des Moines

STATEHOOD: December 28, 1846 (29th)

MOTTO: Our liberties we prize and our rights we will maintain.

POPULATION: 2,869,413 (30th)

AREA: 56,276 sq. mi. (26th)
(145,692 sq km)

HIGHEST POINT: 1,670 ft. (Ocheyedan Mound)

LOWEST POINT: 480 ft. (Mississippi River)

FLOWER: Wild rose

TREE: Oak

BIRD: Eastern goldfinch

Iowa

Iowa's greatest resource is its fertile soil. Like that in the rest of the midwestern farm belt, Iowa's soil was deposited by glaciers that once covered the entire state. Now farms cover 87 percent of the land, producing one fifth of the nation's corn and about one quarter of its hogs.

Following a national trend, farms in Iowa have been increasing in size while decreasing in number. The cause of this has been large agricultural corporations buying up and merging small family spreads. In 1955, there were 193,000 farms in Iowa; today, there are merely half that number. Many small farmers, unable to compete, have gone bankrupt, and their failures have threatened Iowa's small-town way of life. One way that the state has sought to stabilize its economy during bad farm cycles has been to encourage nonfarm industries, such as computer manufacturing in Cedar Rapids and insurance in Des Moines.

Most people think of Iowa as pancake flat, and central Iowa certainly is, but other parts of the state are hilly. In the northeastern corner, for instance, streams have eroded the bedrock to form rugged valleys. In fact, some of the bluffs lining the Mississippi River are four hundred feet (120 m) high. In the west, however, the hills bordering the Missouri River Valley aren't uneroded bedrock but accumulations of windblown silt called loess.

Because Iowa is a state of small towns, it can't support the same cultural institutions, such as symphonies and museums, that states with large cities can. Instead, cultural life in Iowa is often centered on colleges and universities, such as the University of Iowa, which runs the prestigious Iowa Writers' Workshop.

The Uniform State

Because Iowa has an evenly distributed population and very few minorities (only 4 percent of the population), social scientists often use it as an example of "large-scale uniformity." This means that, compared to other states, Iowans are very much alike.

Each of Iowa's small towns is often little more than a few houses, some grain elevators, and a church. Most Iowans say they prefer life on that scale. Yet more and more have been forced by farm failures to take jobs in the cities.

LEGEND

Interstate Highways	State Capital	Native American Reservations	National Forests	National Parks and Refuges	Highest Point	0 miles 50 / 0 kilometers 80

Isle Royale National Park

LAKE SUPERIOR

Copper Harbor •

Houghton •

L'Anse Reservation

Ironwood •
Lake Gogebic
Michigamme Reservoir
MONTREAL R.

Marquette

MICHIGAMME R.

BRULE R.

Iron Mountain •

MENOMINEE R.

Escanaba •

Menominee •

Pictured Rocks National Lakeshore

TAHQUAMENON R.

Manistique •

Manistique Lake

Sault Ste. Marie •

CANADA

Drummond Island

Mackinac Island

Cheboygan •

Petosky •

Alpena •

Hubbard Lake

DID YOU KNOW?
that Lake Superior is the largest body of freshwater in the world?

LAKE HURON

WISCONSIN

Beaver Island

N. Manitou Island
S. Manitou Island

Sleeping Bear Dunes National Lakeshore

Traverse City •

Higgins Lake

Houghton Lake

Houghton Lake •

Manistee •

Isabella Reservation

Midland •

Harbor Beach •

Bay City •

Mount Pleasant •

Saginaw •

The Motor City
The U.S. auto industry began in Detroit and the nearby cities of Dearborn, Flint, and Lansing. When Americans began buying more foreign cars during the 1980s, the auto plants in and around Detroit suffered. Yet the area remains home to America's three largest car companies.

LAKE MICHIGAN

Muskegon •
Grand Haven •

MUSKEGON RIVER

Grand Rapids

GRAND RIVER

Flint

Port Huron •

Milwaukee •

Holland •

ST. CLAIR R.

★ **Lansing**

Detroit

Lake St. Clair

Dearborn •

Windsor

Kalamazoo •

Battle Creek •

Ann Arbor •

DETROIT R.

Chicago •

ST. JOSEPH RIVER

IL.

Gary •

INDIANA

OHIO

Toledo •

LAKE ERIE

← 400 miles (644 km) →

ABOUT MICHIGAN

NICKNAME: Wolverine State

CAPITAL: Lansing

STATEHOOD: January 26, 1837 (26th)

MOTTO: If you seek a beautiful peninsula, look around you.

POPULATION: 9,863,775 (8th)

AREA: 96,705 sq. mi. (11th)
(250,358 sq km)

HIGHEST POINT: 1,979 ft. (Mount Arvon)

LOWEST POINT: 571 ft. (Lake Erie)

FLOWER: Apple blossom

TREE: White pine

BIRD: Robin

FISH: Brook trout

Michigan

A peninsula is a spit of land, shaped like a tongue, bounded on three sides by water. The state of Michigan is actually a pair of peninsulas, one divided from the other by the Straits of Mackinac (pronounced MACK-i-naw). Michigan's sometimes hilly, sometimes swampy Upper Peninsula is connected to the flatter, mitten-shaped Lower Peninsula by the Mackinac Bridge.

Michigan is called the Great Lakes State because it borders four of the five Great Lakes. As a result, shipping has always been an important business there. The locks at Sault Ste. Marie (nicknamed "the Soo") were opened in 1855 to service ships carrying timber and iron ore from Minnesota and the Upper Peninsula. These locks, which equalize the water level between Lake Superior and Lake Huron, are still among the world's busiest.

Michiganders in great numbers also use the Great Lakes for recreation. The rural Upper Peninsula doesn't have many people, but most of them fish. So do the carloads of Detroiters and Chicagoans who visit the Upper Peninsula each summer for a vacation out-of-doors. Despite the fact that it contains every one of Michigan's major cities and important industrial centers, the Lower Peninsula is no less outdoorsy. In fact, Michiganders of both peninsulas own more boats than residents of any other state.

The fish boil has been a Great Lakes tradition since the nineteenth century. It was devised by Scandinavian immigrants who wanted an easy way to cook whitefish and lake trout. For a traditional outdoor fish boil, Michiganders cook chunks of fish, potatoes, and onions in seasoned water over large wood fires.

75%

Michigan's Slice of the Pie

Michigan produces about 75 percent of the sour pie cherries grown in the United States. The area around Traverse City is particularly good for growing cherries because Lake Michigan moderates the weather there, tempering the frosts and cooling the orchards during summer.

Large ships haul cargo from the Midwest to the East (and beyond) using the St. Lawrence Seaway. This system of canals, locks, and dams joins the Great Lakes to the Atlantic Ocean.

LEGEND

Interstate Highways	State Capital	Native American Reservations	National Forests	National Parks and Refuges	Marshlands	Highest Point		miles	50
20	★					▲	0	kilometers	80

The Mesabi Range once produced more than half the world's iron ore. The richest deposits have long been depleted, but the area around Hibbing still fills about 80 percent of the U.S. need with a plentiful low-grade ore called taconite. Mining companies get at the taconite by stripping away the thin soil and digging large open pits.

CANADA

Lake of the Woods

Voyageurs National Park

Red Lake Reservation

International Falls

Rainy Lake

Grand Portage Reservation

Mud Lake

RED RIVER

Upper Red Lake

Thief River Falls

Lower Red Lake

Bois Forte Reservation

Vermillion Lake

Crookston

Bemidji

Lake Winnibigoshish

MESABI RANGE

LAKE SUPERIOR

White Earth Reservation

Leech Lake

Hibbing

Duluth

NORTH DAKOTA

Fargo · Moorhead

Leech Lake Reservation

MISSISSIPPI RIVER

Superior

MICH.

OTTER TAIL R.

Otter Tail Lake

Fond du Lac Reservation

BOIS DE SIOUX R.

Brainerd

Mille Lacs Lake

35

Fergus Falls

ST. CROIX RIVER

Lake Traverse

94

Alexandria

WISCONSIN

St. Cloud

Big Stone Lake

SOUTH DAKOTA

Wilmar

Minneapolis

MINNESOTA R.

St. Paul ★

94

Marshall

New Ulm

Mankato

35

MISSISSIPPI RIVER

BLUE EARTH R.

Owatonna

Winona

Rochester

Worthington

90

Albert Lea

90

Sioux Falls ·

DID YOU KNOW?

that Minnesota has long since run out of new names for lakes? (For example, there are 201 Mud Lakes and 154 Long Lakes.)

IOWA

◄———————— 358 miles (576 km) ————————►

ABOUT MINNESOTA

NICKNAME: Gopher State

CAPITAL: St. Paul

STATEHOOD: May 11, 1858 (32nd)

MOTTO: Star of the North.

POPULATION: 4,775,508 (21st)

AREA: 86,943 sq. mi. (12th)
(225,085 sq km)

HIGHEST POINT: 2,301 ft. (Eagle Mountain)

LOWEST POINT: 600 ft. (Lake Superior)

FLOWER: Pink and white lady's sli

TREE: Norway pine

BIRD: Common loon

FISH: Walleye

Minnesota

Half of Minnesota's population lives in or near the Twin Cities of Minneapolis and St. Paul, built along the Mississippi River at the head of its navigable waters. Indeed, the Twin Cities are the largest metropolitan area for hundreds of miles around. As a result, they've become an important transportation, business, and cultural center for the entire upper Midwest.

Minneapolis and St. Paul are such cosmopolitan cities that a minority presence there doesn't seem unusual, yet that isn't the case elsewhere in Minnesota. Overwhelmingly, Minnesota's residents are white, mostly of German and Scandinavian descent, accounting for 93 percent of the population statewide. Even in a city such as Duluth, all the minorities taken together account for just 4 percent of the population.

Minnesota calls itself the Land of Ten Thousand Lakes, even though there are more than fifteen thousand of them. Most were left behind when the midwestern glaciers receded after the last Ice Age. In the Mesabi Range, those glaciers bulldozed away rock covering large iron ore deposits. Elsewhere, they dumped the same rich soil that makes Iowa farmland so fertile. Not surprisingly, mining and dairying have both become important industries in the state. Minnesota's dairy cows rank among the national leaders in butter production, while Duluth remains one of the world's busiest freshwater ports, largely because of iron ore and grain shipments.

What most Americans know about Minnesota, true or not, they probably learned from Garrison Keillor, host of *A Prairie Home Companion.* Keillor's weekly radio variety show, broadcast live from St. Paul, features "The News from Lake Wobegon," an account of recent events in Keillor's imaginary hometown "where all the children are above average."

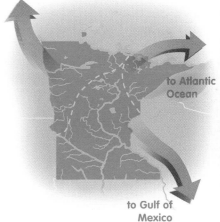

to Hudson Bay

to Atlantic Ocean

to Gulf of Mexico

Minnesota straddles three continental watersheds. Southern Minnesota drains into the Mississippi River (and thereby the Gulf of Mexico). In the west, the Red River flows north toward Canada's Hudson Bay. In the northeast, the region around Duluth drains into the Atlantic Ocean via Lake Superior.

Canoeing is particularly popular in Minnesota, especially along the upper Mississippi River. The source of the Mississippi can be found at Lake Itasca, near Bemidji.

🛣 20	⭐	⬛	🌲	▲	0 ─── miles ─── 50
Interstate Highways	State Capital	National Parks and Refuges	National Forests	Highest Point	0 ─── kilometers ─── 80

Among the most important of Missouri's diverse industries is the manufacture of transportation equipment. Missourians make automobiles, limousines, railroad cars, aircraft, and even spacecraft. Workers at this factory, for example, assemble fire engines.

IOWA

Squaw Creek National Wildlife Refuge

NEB.

• Maryville

29

35

DES MOINES R.

• Kirksville

CHARITON RIVER

GRAND RIVER

• St. Joseph

MISSOURI RIVER

Hannibal •

ILLINOIS

Springfield

Mark Twain Lake

Topeka

70

Independence

Kansas City

• Sedalia

Columbia

70

35

Jefferson City ⭐

St. Charles

55

70

MISSOURI RIVER

St. Louis

Washington

64

KANSAS

Harry S. Truman Reservoir

Lake of the Ozarks

OSAGE RIVER

MISSISSIPPI RIVER

Nevada

Stockton Lake

44

Rolla •

Farmington

▲

55

Springfield

CURRENT RIVER

Cape Girardeau

Cairo

• Joplin

OZARK MTS.

Big Spring

ST. FRANCIS RIVER

57

OKLAHOMA

Table Rock Lake

Branson •

Bull Shoals Lake

• West Plains

Poplar Bluff

KY.

WHITE RIVER

ARKANSAS

TENN.

DID YOU KNOW?

that the town of Washington is the world's leading manufacturer of corncob pipes?

◄─────── 284 miles (457 km) ───────►

ABOUT MISSOURI

NICKNAME: Show Me State

CAPITAL: Jefferson City

STATEHOOD: August 10, 1821 (24th)

MOTTO: Let the welfare of the people be the supreme law.

POPULATION: 5,468,338 (17th)

AREA: 69,709 sq. mi. (21st) (180,468 sq km)

HIGHEST POINT: 1,772 ft. (Taum Sauk Mt.)

LOWEST POINT: 230 ft. (St. Francis River)

FLOWER: Hawthorn

TREE: Flowering dogwood

BIRD: Bluebird

Missouri

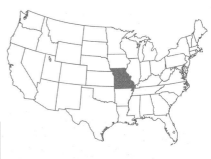

From any map it's easy to tell that the path of the Missouri River determined settlement patterns in the state: St. Louis, for example, was founded near the point at which the Missouri flows into the Mississippi, while Kansas City was built at the junction of the Missouri and Kansas rivers.

River transportation, once the state's most important business, has declined since the end of the nineteenth century, yet St. Louis has remained a national crossroads and midwestern cultural center, home to academically superior Washington University as well as a nationally respected symphony orchestra and art museum. Although the Catholic church in St. Louis isn't as vital as it once was, the city remains important enough to American Catholicism that it recently received a papal visit.

Topographically, Missouri is the most diverse state in the Midwest. The Missouri River marks the southernmost reach of the glaciers that once covered the region. (In fact, the Missouri's channel was carved by glacial meltwater running southeast into the Mississippi.) The land north of the Missouri, with its flattened contours and fertile glacial soil, belongs to the Corn Belt. South of the Missouri rise the forested hills and low mountains of the Ozark Plateau. In western Missouri, the prairies of the Great Plains begin, while in the southeastern corner of the state, in an area called the Bootheel, farmers till the rich bottomlands of the Mississippi floodplain.

Show Me
In 1899, Missouri congressman Willard D. Vandiver told an audience in Philadelphia, "I'm from Missouri. You've got to show me." That attitude of intelligent skepticism was later raised to a mythic level by Independence native President Harry Truman, who kept on his White House desk a famous sign that read, I'M FROM MISSOURI.

27 ft (8 m)

Quite a Big Spring
Underground rivers in the Ozarks have, over time, eaten away large sections of the limestone bedrock, creating some of the biggest springs in the world. Big Spring, the nation's largest, pumps about 11.5 million gallons (43.5 million l) of water into the Current River each hour. That's enough flow to cover a football field with a column of water twenty-seven feet deep.

The 630-foot-tall (192-meter-tall) Gateway Arch celebrates St. Louis's role as the primary nineteenth-century transportation link between the East and the West. Today, St. Louis remains a key trucking and shipping center.

75

LEGEND

🛣 20	⭐	◼	🌲🌲🌲	▲	0 ⟶ miles ⟶ 50	
Interstate Highways	State Capital	National Parks and Refuges	National Forests	Highest Point	0 ⟶ kilometers ⟶ 80	

Every summer, Akron hosts the All-American Soap Box Derby. For more than a century, Akron led the world in tire research and production. Then foreign competitors caught up, and people began buying tires made elsewhere. Akron's city leaders are now searching for another industry to take rubber's place.

Detroit

CANADA

LAKE ERIE

Erie

MICHIGAN

75

80 90 Toledo

Kelleys Island

Ashtabula

Pymatuning Reservoir

Sandusky Lorain **Cleveland** Euclid 90

MAUMEE RIVER Bowling Green 80 90 77 271 CUYAHOGA R. Mosquito Creek Lake

Defiance Findlay Tiffin 71 Kent 80 Warren 80

Fort Wayne SANDUSKY R. Ashland 76 **Akron** Youngstown

75 Lima Mansfield Massillon Canton 76

ST. MARYS R. Indian Lake Marion Millersburg

INDIANA Lake St. Marys GREAT MIAMI RIVER ▲ 71 77 Steubenville PENN.

Springfield **Columbus** ⭐ Newark 77

70 **Dayton** 71 Lancaster Zanesville 70

Middletown 75 Mound City Group National Monument MUSKINGUM RIVER 77

Hamilton Chillicothe Athens OHIO RIVER

Cincinnati SCIOTO RIVER WEST VIRGINIA

71 75 OHIO RIVER Portsmouth

KENTUCKY

DID YOU KNOW?

that the McDonald's in heavily Amish Millersburg has a drive-through window at buggy height?

⟵ 210 miles (338 km) ⟶

ABOUT OHIO

NICKNAME: Buckeye State
CAPITAL: Columbus
STATEHOOD: March 1, 1803 (17th)
MOTTO: With God, all things are possible.

POPULATION: 11,256,654 (7th)
AREA: 44,828 sq. mi. (34th) (116,054 sq km)
HIGHEST POINT: 1,549 ft. (Campbell Hill)
LOWEST POINT: 455 ft. (Ohio River)

FLOWER: Scarlet carnation
TREE: Buckeye
BIRD: Cardinal

Ohio

Ohio is easy to cross, which is why most nineteenth-century pioneers passed through it on their journeys west. The state contains no natural barriers, such as deserts or mountain ranges, to make travel difficult. Of course, the Allegheny Plateau, covering eastern Ohio, has some rough hills and deep valleys, but beyond the Scioto River, the rest of the state is just gently rolling farmland. If you prefer water travel, Lake Erie and the Ohio River both provide excellent transportation routes. Every day, ships and barges make extensive use of these waterways, carrying raw materials to (and finished products from) Ohio's many factories. Because of these factories, Ohio ranks second in manufacturing jobs, trailing only California and just ahead of Texas.

Between 1850 and 1950, Ohio's steel and machine-tool industries created good jobs that attracted immigrants from all over the world. Cleveland, for example, has had neighborhoods devoted to Germans, Irish, Poles, Italians, Czechs, Russians, Greeks, and also blacks who moved up from the South after the Civil War. However, as industry in Ohio grew unchecked, so did the presence of black smoke in the air and harmful chemicals in the water. Now that heavy industry in Ohio has declined, as it has elsewhere in the region, Ohioans must contend with the twin problems of pollution and unemployment.

One of the most unusual groups to have settled in Ohio are the Amish. A highly religious people, the Amish are known for their rejection of modern conveniences, such as cars and electricity, and for their excellent farming skills. Although many Amish live in Pennsylvania, the nation's largest Amish community is located in Holmes County near Millersburg.

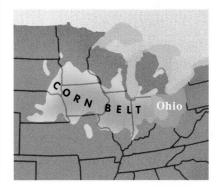

Ohio lies at the eastern end of the agricultural Corn Belt stretching west all the way to Nebraska. Known to geographers as the Dissected Till Plains, this region was created thousands of years ago by glaciers that flattened the land and left behind fertile soil when they melted.

During the 1960s, the pollution became so bad in Lake Erie that it was declared "dead." Since then, environmental laws have stopped the dumping of untreated chemicals. As a result, fish have returned, and beaches have been reopened.

LEGEND

🛣 20 Interstate Highways	✪ State Capital	⬜ Native American Reservations	🌲 National Forests	⬛ National Parks and Refuges	🔺 Highest Point	0 — miles — 50 / 0 — kilometers — 80

DID YOU KNOW?

that Green Bay is known as the Toilet Paper Capital of the World because so many of its paper mills make bathroom tissue?

LAKE SUPERIOR

MICHIGAN

Duluth
Superior
Ashland
Apostle Islands National Lakeshore
MONTREAL R.
Lac du Flambeau Reservation
Bad River Reservation
Lake Chippewa
ST. CROIX RIVER
BRULE RIVER
Iron Mountain
MENOMINEE R.
Lac Courte Oreilles Reservation
CHIPPEWA R.
FLAMBEAU R.
Menominee Reservation
Washington Island
Merrill
Stockbridge Reservation
St. Paul
Marinette
94
River Falls
Eau Claire
BLACK RIVER
Marshfield
Wausau
WOLF RIVER
Oneida Reservation
Sturgeon Bay
Green Bay
Stevens Point
Appleton
Manitowoc
MINNESOTA
Petenwell Lake
39
Oshkosh
Lake Winnebago
Sheboygan
Castle Rock Lake
FOX RIVER
90
La Crosse
Fond du Lac
Beaver Dam
LAKE MICHIGAN
IOWA
WISCONSIN RIVER
Madison
Watertown
43
MISSISSIPPI RIVER
94
Milwaukee
90
Waukesha
Janesville
43
Racine
94
Monroe
Beloit
Kenosha
Dubuque
Rockford
ILLINOIS
Chicago

The German immigrants who came to Milwaukee during the 1840s helped define both the culture and the economy of that city. For example, they brought beer with them, and after the Great Fire destroyed most of Chicago in 1871, Milwaukee's breweries became the nation's most important.

← 295 miles (475 km) →

ABOUT WISCONSIN

NICKNAME: Badger State

CAPITAL: Madison

STATEHOOD: May 29, 1848 (30th)

MOTTO: Forward.

POPULATION: 5,250,446 (18th)

AREA: 65,499 sq. mi. (23rd)
(169,569 sq km)

HIGHEST POINT: 1,951 ft. (Timms Hill)

LOWEST POINT: 579 ft. (Lake Michigan)

FLOWER: Wood violet

TREE: Sugar maple

BIRD: Robin

FISH: Muskellunge

Wisconsin

WISCONSIN
1848

Wisconsin calls itself America's Dairyland with good reason: Its 1.4 million dairy cows are the most of any state. "Milking" this advantage, Wisconsin leads the nation in cheese making and places second (behind California) in butter and overall milk production.

Most of Wisconsin's dairy farms are located in the southern two-thirds of the state. During the last Ice Age, glaciers flattened this area and enriched its soil. Curiously, though, the glaciers flowed around southwestern Wisconsin, creating a Driftless Area of steep valleys and narrow ridges that extends into Minnesota, Iowa, and Illinois. (Drift is glacial debris.) In the north, Wisconsin is mostly forested with second-growth trees that grew up naturally after older ones were cut down by settlers or harvested by paper companies.

Wisconsin's manufacturing industries and largest cities are concentrated in the southeast. The state's most successful paper mills, for example, are in the Fox and Wisconsin river valleys. Southeastern Wisconsin is also filled with many ethnic enclaves that reflect the state's history of heavy immigration from northern Europe. The Germans who arrived first were soon followed by Poles, Swedes, and Norwegians, among other groups. Today, Wisconsinites celebrate their cultural heritage with such annual events as the Wilhelm Tell Festival in New Glarus (Swiss), the Syttende Mai Festival in Stoughton (Norwegian), and the Fyr Bal Festival in Ephraim (Icelandic).

What the Kentucky Derby is to horse racing, the Oshkosh Fly-In is to aviation. Every summer, pilots from all over the world descend on Wittman Regional Airport in Oshkosh, flying more than ten thousand small aircraft. The occasion is the annual convention of the Experimental Aircraft Association.

Nearly 90 percent of the state's milk goes to cheese making, an industry promoted in Wisconsin by German, Swiss, and Norwegian immigrants more than a century ago.

The lakes and forests of Wisconsin's North Woods attract hunters and fishermen from all over the Midwest. Much of the land is protected by Wisconsin's environmental laws, among the most progressive in the nation.

79

YELLOWSTONE RIVER

North Dakota
page 86

South Dakota
page 88

Nebraska
page 84

SOUTH PLATTE RIVER

PLATTE RIVER

MISSOURI RIVER

Kansas
page 82

ARKANSAS RIVER

Great Plains

With no large body of water nearby to moderate the climate, the landlocked states of the Great Plains enjoy (or suffer from) some of the nation's most extreme weather. The summers are hot, the winters are cold and snowy, and the wind blows mightily year-round because there are few natural barriers (such as trees or hills) to block it. During spring and fall when air masses clash overhead, violent weather often results, and tornadoes are common.

LEGEND

Interstate Highways	State Capital	Native American Reservations	National Parks and Refuges	Highest Point	

0	miles	100
0	kilometers	161

DID YOU KNOW?

that the first newspaper in Kansas was published in the Shawnee language?

NEBRASKA

Lincoln

MISSOURI

REPUBLICAN RIVER

Kickapoo Reservation

MISSOURI R.

Lebanon

Waconda Lake

SOLOMON RIVER

Potowatomi Reservation

Tuttle Creek Lake

Atchison

Goodland

SMOKY HILLS

Milford Lake

Manhattan

KANSAS R.

Leavenworth

Kansas City

70

SMOKY HILL RIVER

Hays

SALINE RIVER

Junction City

70

Topeka

Lawrence

Kan. City

Cedar Bluff Reservoir

Salina

Abilene

Olathe

Cheyenne Bottoms

335

Great Bend

McPherson

Emporia

35

John Redmond Reservoir

Garden City

Quivira National Wildlife Refuge

135

Newton

35

Fort Scott

Dodge City

Hutchinson

ARKANSAS RIVER

Cheney Reservoir

Wichita

NEOSHOE RIVER

Ulysses

Pratt

FLINT HILLS

CIMARRON RIVER

RED HILLS

Wellington

Winfield

Liberal

35

Arkansas City

Coffeyville

OKLAHOMA

Tulsa

COL.

Wichita-area companies such as Raytheon and Learjet lead the world in the manufacture of light aircraft, making nearly two out of every three planes sold. Referring to his factory's midcountry location, aircraft executive Walter Beech once said, "No matter where you deliver an airplane from Wichita, you're already halfway there."

← 411 miles (661 km) →

ABOUT KANSAS

NICKNAME: Sunflower State

CAPITAL: Topeka

STATEHOOD: January 29, 1861 (34th)

MOTTO: To the stars through difficulties.

POPULATION: 2,654,052 (32nd)

AREA: 82,282 sq. mi. (15th) (213,018 sq km)

HIGHEST POINT: 4,039 ft. (Mount Sunflower)

LOWEST POINT: 679 ft. (Verdigris River)

FLOWER: Wild native sunflower

TREE: Cottonwood

BIRD: Western meadowlark

Kansas

Kansas seems to encourage misconceptions. For example, early pioneers believed that its dry, hard soil could never be farmed. Yet in 1874, a group of Russian Mennonite immigrants introduced a special strain of hardy winter wheat that required much less water than other wheats. This Turkey Red strain transformed Kansas into the nation's leading wheat producer.

Another misconception is that Kansas is primarily an agricultural state. Once that was true, but modern methods of farming have undermined this small-town way of life—especially the expensive new machinery that allows fewer and fewer people to farm more and more land. Looking elsewhere for work, many young families have left western and central Kansas for the industrialized east. This population shift has left Kansas's small towns smaller and the average age of the people who live in them higher.

Some people even think that Kansas is flat! In fact, much of the state is covered with low hills. The Dissected Till Plains of northeastern Kansas and the Osage Plains in the extreme southeast are both areas of rolling hills and rich prairie soil. West of the Osage Plains are the Flint Hills, whose abundant bluestem grass provides some of the best grazing land in the country. Farther west are the gently rising Great Plains, which take up half the state beginning near Tuttle Creek in the north and Hutchinson in the south.

During the early twentieth century, when William Allen White edited the *Emporia Gazette*, Kansas became internationally famous for its many excellent small-town newspapers. Even today, Kansas has more newspapers per capita than any other state.

Truly Middle America
A limestone monument in a pasture just northeast of Lebanon marks the geographic center of the continental United States. This is the point at which a flat tracing of the country's shape would balance.

Although the wheat fields of central Kansas produce about 20 percent of the annual U.S. harvest, farmers in the state make about twice as much money raising beef cattle in the Flint Hills and elsewhere.

LEGEND

20 Interstate Highways	★ State Capital	Native American Reservations	National Forests	National Parks and Refuges	Grasslands	▲ Highest Point	0 ——— miles ——— 100	0 ——— kilometers ——— 161

DID YOU KNOW?

that Interstate 80, which follows the same route taken by the Oregon Trail and the first transcontinental railroad, remains the nation's busiest east-west highway?

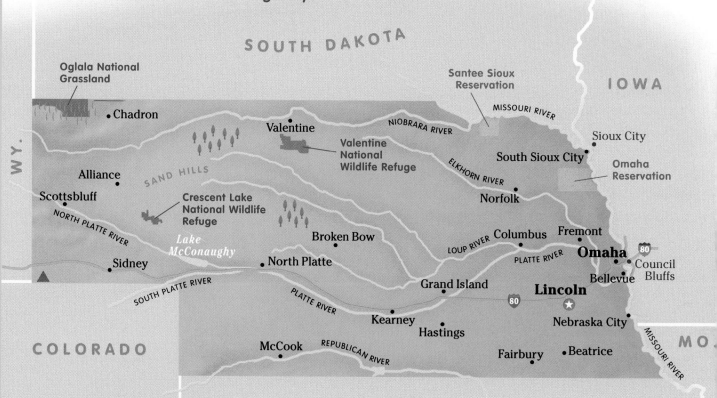

SOUTH DAKOTA

Oglala National Grassland

• Chadron

Santee Sioux Reservation

MISSOURI RIVER

IOWA

Valentine

Valentine National Wildlife Refuge

NIOBRARA RIVER

Sioux City

South Sioux City

ELKHORN RIVER

Omaha Reservation

WY.

Alliance •

SAND HILLS

Norfolk

Scottsbluff •

Crescent Lake National Wildlife Refuge

NORTH PLATTE RIVER

Lake McConaughy

Broken Bow •

LOUP RIVER

Columbus

Fremont

Sidney •

North Platte •

PLATTE RIVER

Omaha

Council Bluffs

Bellevue

Grand Island •

SOUTH PLATTE RIVER

PLATTE RIVER

80

Lincoln ★

COLORADO

Kearney •

Hastings •

Nebraska City

MISSOURI RIVER

MO.

McCook •

REPUBLICAN RIVER

Fairbury •

Beatrice •

KANSAS

Although agriculture remains important to Nebraskans, the state economy has diversified in recent years. For example, Omaha was once a national center for meatpacking. Now the most prosperous companies in town are insurance companies and telemarketers.

◄———————— 415 miles (668 km) ————————►

ABOUT NEBRASKA

NICKNAME: Cornhusker State

CAPITAL: Lincoln

STATEHOOD: March 1, 1867 (37th)

MOTTO: Equality before the law.

POPULATION: 1,666,028 (38th)

AREA: 77,358 sq. mi. (16th)
(200,271 sq km)

HIGHEST POINT: 5,424 ft. (Johnson Township)

LOWEST POINT: 840 ft. (Missouri River)

FLOWER: Goldenrod

TREE: Cottonwood

BIRD: Western meadowlark

Nebraska

The nineteenth-century homesteaders who settled Nebraska came out west to farm. At first, they concentrated themselves in the Platte River Valley, along the route of the Oregon Trail, where water was readily available. Then, as the use of irrigation expanded, they settled other parts of the state, once considered a Great American Desert by early explorers.

Today, agriculture has become such a universal way of life in Nebraska that farms and ranches occupy 96 percent of the land, the highest percentage of any state. In western Nebraska, wheat fields flow uninterrupted to the horizon, while farmers in the east grow corn, the state's best-known and most important crop. Ranching is also profitable in Nebraska, which ranks second behind Texas in beef cattle production.

Nearly all Nebraska lies on the Great Plains, which begin near the junction of the Loup and Platte rivers. (The eastern edge of the state belongs to the Dissected Till Plains.) The terrain, mostly featureless, rises from east to west, but so gradually that it seems flat. Only near the Colorado border does the land give way to the buttes and valleys characteristic of the High Plains. One notable exception are the Sand Hills of north-central Nebraska, the largest sand dune area in North America. The soil there is held in place by grasses that also provide excellent forage for cattle.

They call it Huskermania. The University of Nebraska football team, nicknamed the Cornhuskers, has sold out every one of its home games since November 3, 1962. During those games, Memorial Stadium in Lincoln, seating 72,700 people, becomes—all by itself—the third largest city in the state.

Nebraska's Ogallala Aquifer sits at the northern end of the High Plains Aquifer, the nation's largest underground reservoir. Water pumped from the Ogallala Aquifer allows Nebraska farmers to irrigate more than eight million acres (about 3 million ha), the most irrigated land in any state after California.

The surveyors who laid out Nebraska (and most of the Great Plains) used a strict rectangular grid system. Townships were built up from square 640-acre (259-hectare) "sections," with the basic unit of settlement being the quarter-section farm.

Interstate Highways | **State Capital** | **Native American Reservations** | **National Parks and Refuges** | **Grasslands** | **Highest Point**

| 0 | miles | 100 |
| 0 | kilometers | 161 |

North Dakota typically ranks second behind Kansas in wheat production, yet every few years a particularly good harvest can nudge the state into first place. The two principal varieties grown in North Dakota are hard red spring wheat, used for making bread dough, and durum, from which spaghetti is made.

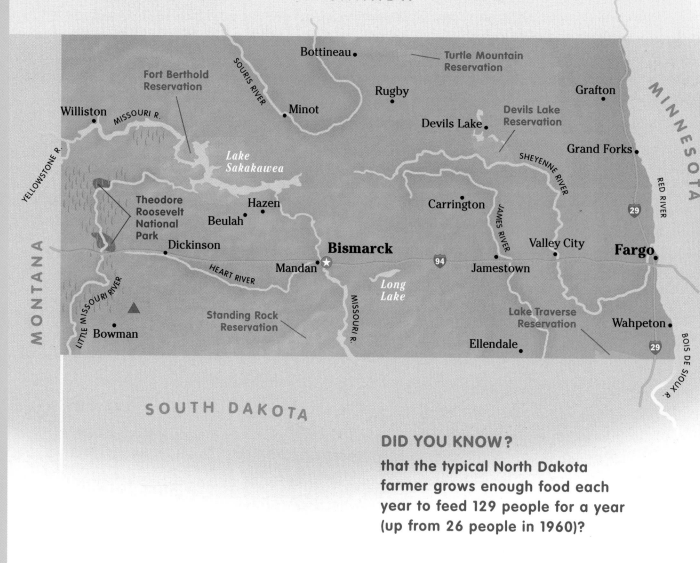

CANADA

Bottineau · — Turtle Mountain Reservation
Fort Berthold Reservation
SOURIS RIVER
Rugby · Grafton ·
Williston Minot · Devils Lake Reservation
MISSOURI R. Devils Lake ·
Lake Sakakawea Grand Forks ·
SHEYENNE RIVER
YELLOWSTONE R.
Theodore Roosevelt National Park Hazen · Carrington · RED RIVER
Beulah · JAMES RIVER
Dickinson · Valley City · Fargo ·
MONTANA LITTLE MISSOURI RIVER HEART RIVER Mandan ☆ **Bismarck** Jamestown · 94
Long Lake MINNESOTA 29
▲ Standing Rock Reservation MISSOURI R. Lake Traverse Reservation Wahpeton ·
Bowman · Ellendale · BOIS DE SIOUX R.
29

SOUTH DAKOTA

DID YOU KNOW?

that the typical North Dakota farmer grows enough food each year to feed 129 people for a year (up from 26 people in 1960)?

←————— 360 miles (579 km) —————→

ABOUT NORTH DAKOTA

NICKNAME: Flickertail State
CAPITAL: Bismarck
STATEHOOD: November 2, 1889 (39th)
MOTTO: Liberty and union, now and forever, one and inseparable.

POPULATION: 633,666 (47th)
AREA: 70,704 sq. mi. (19th) (183,044 sq km)
HIGHEST POINT: 3,506 ft. (White Butte)
LOWEST POINT: 750 ft. (Red River)

FLOWER: Wild prairie rose
TREE: American elm
BIRD: Western meadowlark
FISH: Northern pike

North Dakota

Most North Dakotans have a lively sense of humor about their state. They tell jokes like "You know you're a North Dakotan if you define *summer* as three months of bad sledding." The climate there can indeed be challenging: Far from the moderating influence of an ocean and without trees or hills for windbreaks, North Dakota experiences some of the continent's hottest and coldest temperatures, not to mention frequent dust storms and blizzards. The weather, combined with the state's small population and apparently endless prairie landscape, might make a less hardy people lonely. Yet North Dakotans pride themselves on their positive outlook and spirit of cooperation.

Most of the businesses in the state depend on agriculture. The rich soil supports an abundance of wheat as well as the largest barley, flax, pinto bean, and sunflower crops in the country. Farms tend to be large, nearly three times the national average, which is why North Dakotans live so far apart. The state's tiny manufacturing sector is generally confined to the larger cities, where most of the factories process food—the pasta-making plant in Fargo, for instance, and the sugar beet refineries in Grand Forks.

Fargo and Grand Forks are located in the extremely fertile Red River Valley on the eastern edge of the state. The next regions over are the Drift Prairie and then the Missouri Plateau, a hilly and stony part of the Great Plains that covers the entire western half of North Dakota.

Because so many North Dakotans live in isolated areas, less than half the population has access to a library. To meet this need, most county libraries have established bookmobile programs to service rural areas.

Ice Age glaciers carved North Dakota into a series of stepped plateaus. From the Red River Valley, once the bottom of a huge glacial lake, the land rises sharply to the Drift Prairie (which takes its name from the glacial debris called drift). A similar step separates the Drift Prairie from the Missouri Plateau.

North Dakota has plenty of prairie grass but not much shade. Of the fifty states, it has the lowest percentage of forested land, only about 1 percent. The few trees that do grow there are mostly found in the Turtle Mountains.

LEGEND

Interstate Highways · State Capital · Native American Reservations · National Forests · National Parks and Refuges · Grasslands · Highest Point

| 0 | miles | 100 |
| 0 | kilometers | 161 |

During the early 1980s, Citibank became the single largest employer in Sioux Falls when it moved its credit-card operations there. Since then, other financial services companies have followed, bringing more jobs and transforming Sioux Falls into an important center for credit-card processing.

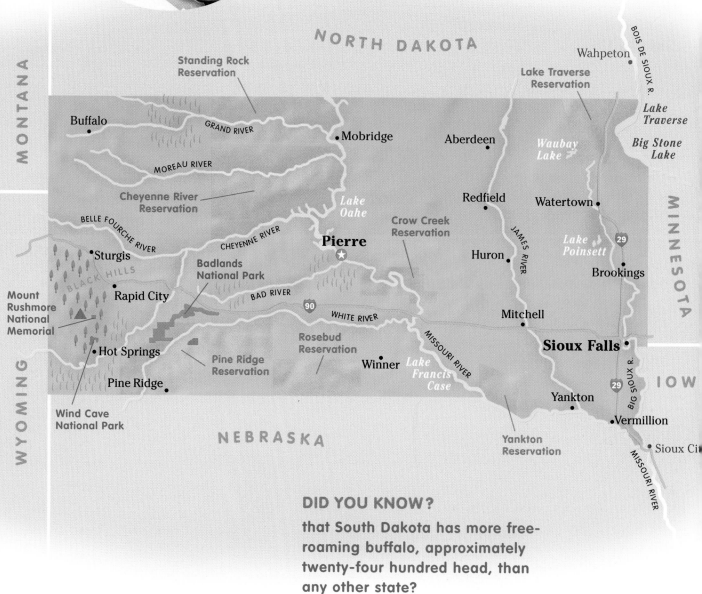

← 380 miles (611 km) →

DID YOU KNOW?

that South Dakota has more free-roaming buffalo, approximately twenty-four hundred head, than any other state?

ABOUT SOUTH DAKOTA

NICKNAME: Mount Rushmore State
CAPITAL: Pierre
STATEHOOD: November 2, 1889 (40th)
MOTTO: Under God the people rule.
POPULATION: 733,133 (46th)
AREA: 77,121 sq. mi. (17th) (199,659 sq km)
HIGHEST POINT: 7,242 ft. (Harney Peak)
LOWEST POINT: 966 ft. (Big Stone Lake)
FLOWER: Pasqueflower
TREE: Black Hills spruce
BIRD: Ring-necked pheasant
FISH: Walleye

South Dakota

South Dakotans seem to live by two simple rules: Where the soil is fertile, you plant crops. Where the grass grows high, you raise livestock. In all, 93 percent of the land in the state is devoted to agriculture. In the fields of the east, farmers grow corn, wheat, hay, and other crops; in the grazing lands of the west, ranchers raise cattle, hogs, and sheep.

The Native Americans who live on the many reservations in South Dakota have never adapted well to this way of life. It may be that because they were once roaming hunters of buffalo, the fixed reservation lifestyle holds little appeal for them. Or, more likely, the condition of the reservation land, some of the worst in the state, has hampered their attempts at agriculture.

Winding among these reservations, the Missouri River is South Dakota's major geographical landmark. East of the river lies the Drift Prairie, where ancient glaciers left behind excellent farmland. Most South Dakotans live on this side of the river, on farms and in small towns.

West of the Missouri, untouched by the glaciers that smoothed the eastern bank, are the dry, treeless grasslands of the Great Plains. Except for the area around the Black Hills, there are so few people in western South Dakota (an average of only three per square mile) that the land seems nearly deserted.

Native Americans, most of them Sioux, make up 7.9 percent of the South Dakota population. (Only Alaska and New Mexico have higher percentages.) Like many other nations, the Oglala Sioux, who live on the Pine Ridge Reservation, hold an annual powwow to celebrate their cultural heritage with craft displays and dancing competitions.

South Dakota has been so successful at promoting itself that tourism now ranks just behind agriculture in the state economy. One of the most popular sights is the quartet of presidential busts carved into the Black Hills at Mount Rushmore. Each head stands as tall as a six-story building.

Rising above southwestern South Dakota is a range of granite cliffs. The Sioux call this land Paha Sapa. Whites call it the Black Hills because thick pine forests make the region look much darker than the surrounding plain.

CANADA

MISSOURI RIVER

Montana
page 96

YELLOWSTONE RIVER

Idaho
page 94

SNAKE RIVER

Wyoming
page 100

NORTH PLATTE RIVER

Utah
page 98

Colorado
page 92

SOUTH PLATTE RIVER

COLORADO RIVER

RIO GRANDE

ARKANSAS RIVER

MEXICO

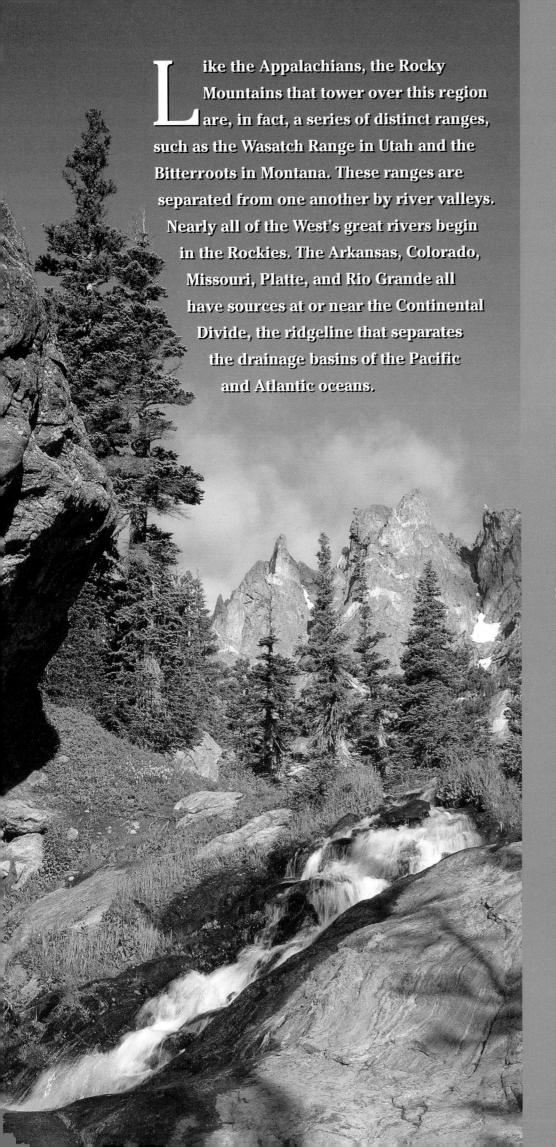

L ike the Appalachians, the Rocky Mountains that tower over this region are, in fact, a series of distinct ranges, such as the Wasatch Range in Utah and the Bitterroots in Montana. These ranges are separated from one another by river valleys. Nearly all of the West's great rivers begin in the Rockies. The Arkansas, Colorado, Missouri, Platte, and Rio Grande all have sources at or near the Continental Divide, the ridgeline that separates the drainage basins of the Pacific and Atlantic oceans.

Mountain

LEGEND

 Interstate Highways   State Capital   Native American Reservations   National Forests   National Parks and Refuges   Grasslands   Highest Point

0	miles	100
0	kilometers	161

Colorado Springs, the home of the Air Force Academy, is the center of the state's robust defense and aerospace industries. Just south of town, for example, inside hollowed-out Cheyenne Mountain, the North American Aerospace Defense Command (NORAD) monitors U.S. and Canadian airspace for incoming aircraft and missiles.

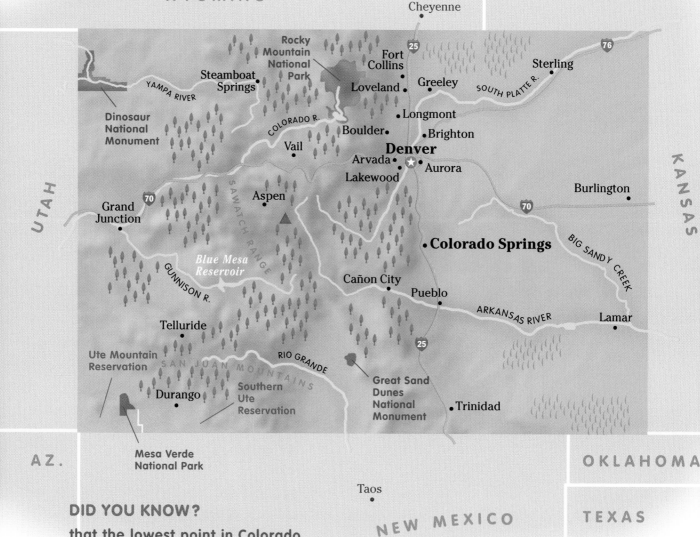

DID YOU KNOW?

that the lowest point in Colorado is higher than the highest point in eighteen states?

387 miles (623 km)

ABOUT COLORADO

NICKNAME: Centennial State
CAPITAL: Denver
STATEHOOD: August 1, 1876 (38th)
MOTTO: Nothing without providence.

POPULATION: 4,056,133 (24th)
AREA: 104,100 sq. mi. (8th)
(269,503 sq km)
HIGHEST POINT: 14,433 ft. (Mount Elbert)
LOWEST POINT: 3,350 ft. (Arkansas River)

FLOWER: Rocky Mountain columbine
TREE: Blue spruce
BIRD: Lark bunting

Colorado

More than in other states, the culture wars of the late twentieth and early twenty-first centuries are being fought in Colorado. On one side are highly conservative old-time Coloradans led by the Coors family of brewing fame. On the other are more recent immigrants, including many liberals from California. Lately, the hottest topics have been the Rocky Mountains (whether they should be mined or protected), military spending, and gay rights.

The Rockies still support a profitable mining industry, and cattle ranches still cover the High Plains, yet the state's economy no longer depends so heavily on natural resources. Instead, as Colorado has become more cosmopolitan, its economy has diversified, and light manufacturing—of scientific instruments, for example—has flourished.

Colorado's recent economic boom has particularly focused on the string of cities, from Pueblo north to Fort Collins, lining the eastern foothills of the Rockies. Most of the new money has concentrated here, as well as three quarters of the state's population.

Although Colorado is closely identified with the southern Rockies, much of the state happens to be flat. The eastern two-fifths belongs to the Great Plains, which rise gently from the Kansas border. The Rockies take up the central two-fifths, while the western fringe sits atop the Colorado Plateau. Wind and water have eroded this upland into a scenic maze of canyons and flat-topped hills called mesas.

Each winter, twelve million people visit Colorado's world-famous ski resorts. Among the most glamorous of these are Aspen and Vail. (Vail also happens to be the largest ski resort in North America.) Thanks to state-of-the-art snowmaking machines, the ski season begins as early as October and continues for eight months.

	COLORADO IN CROSS SECTION
14,000 ft. / 4,267 m	
12,000 ft. / 3,658 m	
10,000 ft. / 3,048 m	
8,000 ft. / 2,438 m	
	Mean Altitude: 6,800 ft. / 2,073 m
6,000 ft. / 1,829 m	
4,000 ft. / 1,219 m	
2,000 ft. / 610 m	

Rocky Mountain High
Colorado's mean altitude of sixty-eight hundred feet is the highest of any state. Nationwide, there are ninety-one peaks above fourteen thousand feet. Of these ninety-one "fourteeners," fifty-six are in Colorado.

With Colorado's growth, Denver has become the transportation and financial center of the Mountain West. It's called the Mile High City because it sits at an average elevation of 5,280 feet (1,609 m).

Interstate Highways	State Capital	Native American Reservations	National Forests	National Parks and Refuges	Highest Point	0 — miles — 100	
						0 — kilometers — 161	

CANADA

Priest Lake

Sandpoint

Lake Pend Oreille

WASH.

Spokane

Coeur d'Alene

Kellog

90

Coeur d'Alene Reservation

Moscow

CLEARWATER RIVER

Missoula

Lewiston

Nez Perce Reservation

S. FORK CLEARWATER

SELWAY RIVER

Butte

DID YOU KNOW?

Grangeville

CLEARWATER R.

CLEARWATER MTS.

SALMON RIVER

MONTANA

that the wiggle in Idaho's otherwise straight western border is Hells Canyon, the continent's deepest river-carved gorge?

SALMON RIVER MTS.

Salmon

SNAKE RIVER

SAWTOOTH MTS.

Yellowstone National Park

Craters of the Moon National Monument

15

Rexburg

Caldwell

Sun Valley

Ketchum

Nampa

Hailey

Idaho Falls

★ **Boise**

Mountain Home

SNAKE RIVER PLAIN

Grays Lake

WYO.

OREGON

84

American Falls Reservoir

Fort Hall Reservation

Duck Valley Reservation

86

Pocatello

Twin Falls

Burley

15

84

Bear Lake

Preston

NEVADA

UTAH

Logan

305 miles (491 km)

Clear Springs Foods, headquartered near Twin Falls, is the world's leading producer of aqua-cultured rainbow trout. Altogether, companies in south-central Idaho produce about 75 percent of the food-size trout sold in the United States. The fish are raised in ponds cooled by underground springs.

ABOUT IDAHO

NICKNAME: Gem State

CAPITAL: Boise

STATEHOOD: July 3, 1890 (43rd)

MOTTO: Let it be perpetual.

POPULATION: 1,251,700 (40th)

AREA: 83,574 sq. mi. (14th) (216,363 sq km)

HIGHEST POINT: 12,662 ft. (Borah Peak)

LOWEST POINT: 710 ft. (Snake River)

FLOWER: Syringa

TREE: Western white pine

BIRD: Mountain bluebird

FISH: Cutthroat trout

Idaho

The Idaho Potato Commission spends bushels of money each year to make sure that *Idaho* and *potato* remain closely linked in the American mind. "Dice 'em, hash 'em, boil 'em, mash 'em!" is a popular football cheer. Yet even more important is the fact that the Idaho potato industry generates $2.5 billion a year, or 15 percent of the state's gross product, which is no small potatoes.

Still, to dismiss Idaho as a single giant potato farm would be wrong. For one thing, the potato farms are crammed into just one small section of the state, the Snake River Plain, Idaho's only level ground. Elsewhere, the state is a wilderness of forests and mountains, including some of the country's most rugged and least accessible land. Residents of the Panhandle, in particular, tend to be independent and self-reliant, because they have to be.

Although Idaho, like most mountain states, has some mineral and timber resources, environmentally conscious residents are much more interested in developing the state's wilderness tourism industry. For example, thanks to federal protection, the Salmon and Clearwater rivers have both become meccas for white-water rafters.

Except for isolated timber and mining settlements, most towns in Idaho follow the course of the Snake River, and most people live on the Snake River Plain atop the Columbia Plateau. Aside from a lip of the Great Basin jutting into the state from Utah, the rest of Idaho—specifically, the northern two-thirds—belongs to the Rocky Mountains.

At the World Center for Birds of Prey in Boise, the Peregrine Fund houses over two hundred endangered hunting birds, including California condors, harpy eagles, and Aplomado falcons. An international leader in endangered species research, the center breeds these birds in captivity, then releases their young into the wild.

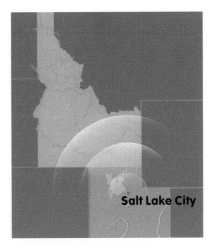

Salt Lake City

After Utah, Idaho has the highest concentration of Mormons, or members of the Church of Jesus Christ of Latter-day Saints. Statewide, Mormons make up about 27 percent of the population. However, near the Utah border in Idaho's desert southeast, many towns are as much as 90 percent Mormon.

Idaho boasts eighteen million acres (about 7 million ha) of wilderness, the most of any state after Alaska. In fact, some parts of the mountainous, heavily forested Panhandle have remained essentially unchanged since Lewis and Clark explored them in 1805.

LEGEND

20	⭐	◻	🌲	◼	▲	0	miles	100
Interstate Highways	State Capital	Native American Reservations	National Forests	National Parks and Refuges	Highest Point	0	kilometers	161

Nearly all the manufacturing in Montana makes use of the state's natural resources. For example, lumber and wood products such as pencils and telephone poles account for about one third of the state's total output. The rest are mostly oil, coal, metal, and food products.

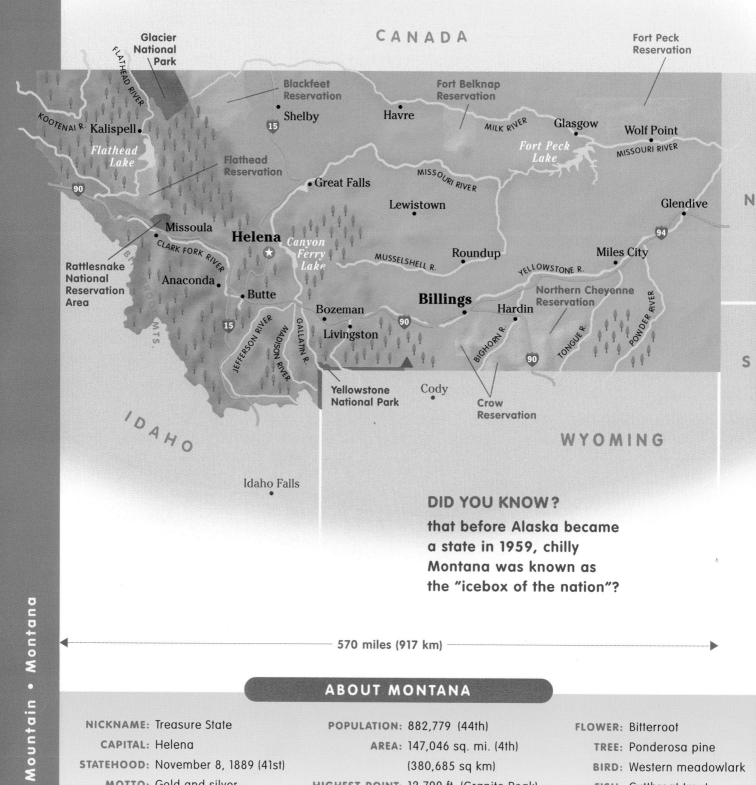

CANADA

Glacier National Park

Fort Peck Reservation

Blackfeet Reservation

Fort Belknap Reservation

FLATHEAD RIVER

KOOTENAI R. Kalispell

Shelby

Havre

MILK RIVER

Glasgow

Wolf Point

MISSOURI RIVER

Flathead Lake

15

Fort Peck Lake

Flathead Reservation

Great Falls

MISSOURI RIVER

90

Lewistown

Glendive

N

Missoula

Helena ⭐

Canyon Ferry Lake

MUSSELSHELL R.

Roundup

Miles City

94

CLARK FORK RIVER

Rattlesnake National Reservation Area

Anaconda

YELLOWSTONE R.

S.

Butte

15

Billings

Hardin

Northern Cheyenne Reservation

POWDER RIVER

BITTERROOT MTS.

JEFFERSON RIVER

MADISON RIVER

GALLATIN R.

Bozeman

90

Livingston

BIGHORN R.

TONGUE R.

90

Yellowstone National Park

Cody

Crow Reservation

IDAHO

WYOMING

Idaho Falls

DID YOU KNOW?

that before Alaska became a state in 1959, chilly Montana was known as the "icebox of the nation"?

570 miles (917 km)

ABOUT MONTANA

NICKNAME: Treasure State

CAPITAL: Helena

STATEHOOD: November 8, 1889 (41st)

MOTTO: Gold and silver.

POPULATION: 882,779 (44th)

AREA: 147,046 sq. mi. (4th)
(380,685 sq km)

HIGHEST POINT: 12,799 ft. (Granite Peak)

LOWEST POINT: 1,800 ft. (Kootenai River)

FLOWER: Bitterroot

TREE: Ponderosa pine

BIRD: Western meadowlark

FISH: Cutthroat trout

Montana

There are so few Montanans that parts of the state, the fourth largest, seem uninhabited. Attracted by this solitude, more and more celebrities have been buying ranches there to get away from it all. Meanwhile, the people who live there don't seem to take much notice. They're mostly cattle ranchers and wheat farmers, though a good number work for mining companies. The state's gold, silver, and copper supplies have largely run out, but oil, coal, and natural gas have taken their place.

As oil and coal mining have expanded, they've become more controversial, especially among Montana's Native Americans. (The second largest group after whites, they make up 6 percent of the state's population.) Most Native Americans living on Montana reservations urgently need the jobs and income mining would provide. However, many reservation leaders worry that exploiting these resources might permanently damage the environment.

Montana is called Big Sky Country because in the eastern two thirds of the state, where the land is flat and open, it's easy to see a lot of sky. Buttes and small mountain ranges occasionally interrupt this treeless Great Plains grassland, yet these seem insignificant compared to the Rocky Mountains of western Montana. Along the backbone of the Rockies runs the Continental Divide. In general, rain that falls on the western side of this divide runs into the Pacific Ocean, while rain that falls on its eastern side drains into the Atlantic.

Life in Montana is strongly oriented toward the outdoors. One reason is that Montanans, who tend to live far away from one another, don't want to get "cabin fever." Another is that the hunting and fishing there are exceptional: The Yellowstone River, for example, offers some of the best fly fishing in the world.

Chinook Winds

Chinooks are unusually warm, dry winds that blow down from the Rockies every so often during winter. They can raise the air temperature 40°F (22°C) in less than an hour and melt enough snow so that cattle can graze— at least until the next snowfall.

Western Montana includes some of the most difficult and out-of-the-way territory in the country. There are mountains in Glacier National Park so steep and remote that no one has ever climbed them.

Interstate Highways

State Capital

Native American Reservations

National Forests

National Parks and Refuges

Highest Point

| 0 | miles | 100 |
| 0 | kilometers | 161 |

The federal government does a lot of its rocket shopping in Utah. The most important of its contractors there is the Thiokol Corporation, the world's largest producer of rocket engines. Thiokol makes reusable engines for the space shuttle as well as the motors used to launch Trident II and Minuteman nuclear missiles.

IDAHO

Bear Lake

BEAR R.

84 15

Logan

Brigham City

WYOMING

Ogden

Great Salt Lake

84 80

BONNEVILLE SALT FLATS

Salt Lake City

UINTA MOUNTAINS

80

Sandy

Tooele

Orem

Dinosaur National Monument

Goshute Reservation

Provo

Utah Lake

Uintah and Ouray Reservation

COLORADO

NEVADA

GREAT SALT LAKE DESERT

SEVIER DESERT

15

Price

Ely

Delta

SEVIER RIVER

WASATCH RANGE

GREEN RIVER

Grand Junction

Richfield

70

Moab

Arches National Park

SAN RAFAEL DESERT

Canyonlands National Park

Cedar City

Bryce Canyon National Park

COLORADO RIVER

Blanding

St. George

Zion National Park

SAN JUAN RIVER

Navajo Reservation

MONUMENT VALLEY

Lake Powell

N.M.

DID YOU KNOW?

that the Mormon church originally wanted to call the state Deseret, a name from the Book of Mormon that means "land of honeybees"?

ARIZONA

275 miles (442 km)

ABOUT UTAH

NICKNAME: Beehive State

CAPITAL: Salt Lake City

STATEHOOD: January 4, 1896 (45th)

MOTTO: Industry.

POPULATION: 2,129,836 (34th)

AREA: 84,904 sq. mi. (13th)
(219,806 sq km)

HIGHEST POINT: 13,528 ft. (Kings Peak)

LOWEST POINT: 2,000 ft. (Beaverdam Wash)

FLOWER: Sego lily

TREE: Blue spruce

BIRD: California gull

FISH: Bonneville cutthroat trout

Utah

The U.S. Constitution demands a separation between church and state. Yet it's difficult to imagine Utah without the Mormon church, also known as the Church of Jesus Christ of Latter-day Saints. A group of Mormons led by Brigham Young settled Utah in 1847, and Mormons still make up 70 percent of the population. Although the Mormon church no longer governs the state, it continues to play an important role in Utah's social life and institutions. For example, the Mormon preference for large families has kept the Utah birthrate well above the national average.

The Mormons were allowed to claim Utah, the nation's second driest state (after Nevada), largely because no other settlers wanted it. Most of the land, though geologically spectacular, cannot be farmed. What little arable land there is sits in a narrow band at the foot of the Wasatch Mountains, where streams fed by snowmelt carry water and mineral sediments down from the Rockies. As a result, about 75 percent of the population lives along the Wasatch Front between Provo and Ogden.

In the Rockies, the biggest business is mining, primarily gold, silver, and lead. To the south and east, the mountains flatten out into the Colorado Plateau, which covers slightly more than half the state. In this scenic region, featuring Zion and Bryce Canyon national parks, tourism is the most important industry. The western third of Utah belongs to the Great Basin and contains the Sevier and Great Salt Lake deserts as well as some of the flattest land on the continent.

Among Christians, Mormons are remarkable for having many beliefs uniquely their own, including their emphasis on business. To finance extensive missionary activities, the Mormon church runs many for-profit companies, including a department-store chain, an insurance company, and a tuna factory in San Diego.

The Great Salt Lake is all that's left of a huge freshwater lake that once covered western Utah. This ancient body of water, Lake Bonneville, was about the size that Lake Michigan is today. However, when the surrounding land rose, Lake Bonneville dried up, leaving the Great Salt Lake behind.

Southern Utah boasts some of the most spectacular rock formations on the North American continent. The buttes of Monument Valley may look familiar because they've appeared in many classic Hollywood westerns.

LEGEND

 Interstate Highways
 State Capital
Native American Reservations
National Forests
National Parks and Refuges
Grasslands
Highest Point

| 0 | | miles | | 100 |
| 0 | | kilometers | | 161 |

Oil is the most valuable mineral in Wyoming, which produces about ninety million barrels of crude each year. This amount ranks the state fourth nationally behind Texas, Louisiana, and California. Many economists believe that Wyoming's future will depend increasingly on mining, particularly its reserves of oil, coal, and natural gas.

MONTANA

Yellowstone National Park

YELLOWSTONE R.

Powell

Cody

Yellowstone Lake

BIGHORN RIVER

BIG HORN MOUNTAINS

Sheridan

POWDER RIVER

90

Buffalo

Gillette

Grand Teton National Park

Jackson

SNAKE RIVER

Wind River Reservation

Worland

WIND RIVER

WIND RIVER RANGE

Thermopolis

BELLE FOURCHE RIVER

90

Newcastle

25

Riverton

Lander

SWEETWATER RIVER

Casper

Douglas

NORTH PLATTE RIVER

MEDICINE BOW MOUNTAINS

LARAMIE R.

Torrington

IDAHO

Kemmerer

GREEN RIVER

Pathfinder Reservoir

GREAT DIVIDE BASIN

Seminoe Reservoir

Rawlins

MEDICINE BOW R.

Wheatland

Green River

Rock Springs

80

Laramie

Cheyenne

80

Evanston

Flaming Gorge Reservoir

25

NEBRASKA

SOUTH DAKOTA

UTAH

COLORADO

Denver

DID YOU KNOW?

that the 308-foot (94-meter) Lower Falls of the Yellowstone River is twice the height of Niagara Falls?

365 miles (587 km)

ABOUT WYOMING

NICKNAME: Equality State
CAPITAL: Cheyenne
STATEHOOD: July 10, 1890 (44th)
MOTTO: Equal rights.

POPULATION: 479,602 (50th)
AREA: 97,818 sq. mi. (10th)
(253,239 sq km)
HIGHEST POINT: 13,804 ft. (Gannett Peak)
LOWEST POINT: 3,099 ft. (Belle Fourche River)

FLOWER: Indian paintbrush
TREE: Plains cottonwood
BIRD: Meadowlark
FISH: Cutthroat trout

Wyoming

Famous for its scenic beauty, Wyoming attracts more than seven million tourists each year. Many come to visit Yellowstone and Grand Teton national parks, yet few stay. The population of Wyoming, despite its large size, is the lowest of any state in the Union, perhaps because life on its dry plains and in its rugged mountains can be so intimidating.

Most of the people who live in Wyoming are the descendants of the whites, Mexicans, and Native Americans who originally settled the land. The state's many ranches and rodeos give the impression that Wyoming is the last refuge of the American cowboy. In fact, many Wyoming ranchers have to hire cowboys from Mexico, Chile, and Peru to do this hard, lonesome work.

Ranching and other farming activities generate $1.5 billion a year for Wyoming, yet agriculture ranks a distant third in the state economy. Mining is far and away Wyoming's biggest business, at $3.5 billion per year (with tourism second). In addition to its plentiful oil, Wyoming has huge coal reserves, the nation's largest, enough to last more than three hundred years.

Only the eastern fringe of Wyoming lies on the Great Plains. The rest of the state, which straddles the Continental Divide, belongs to the Rocky Mountains. Separating Wyoming's many ranges are the dry flatlands of the Intermontane Basin. Much of Wyoming's mineral wealth rests beneath these high, cold plateaus, whose short-grass prairies provide excellent grazing for the state's largest cattle ranches.

Cheyenne began hosting its annual Frontier Days celebration in 1897. The rodeo was the brainchild of a Union Pacific railroad agent who wanted to promote his trains but needed a destination. Today, more than twelve hundred cowboys and cowgirls take part in the roping, riding, and steer-wrestling competitions.

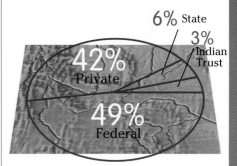

6% State
3% Indian Trust
42% Private
49% Federal

The federal government still owns a great deal of land in the West. For example, it owns 49 percent of Wyoming and more than half of western Montana.

Although Wyoming has few people, its cattle and sheep populations are huge. In all, rangeland covers a whopping 82 percent of Wyoming, the highest percentage of any state.

Nevada
page 106

COLORADO RIVER

ARKANSAS RIVER

Oklahoma
page 110

Arizona
page 104

New
Mexico
page 108

RED RIVER

Texas
page 112

RIO GRANDE

MEXICO

PACIFIC OCEAN

GULF OF MEXICO

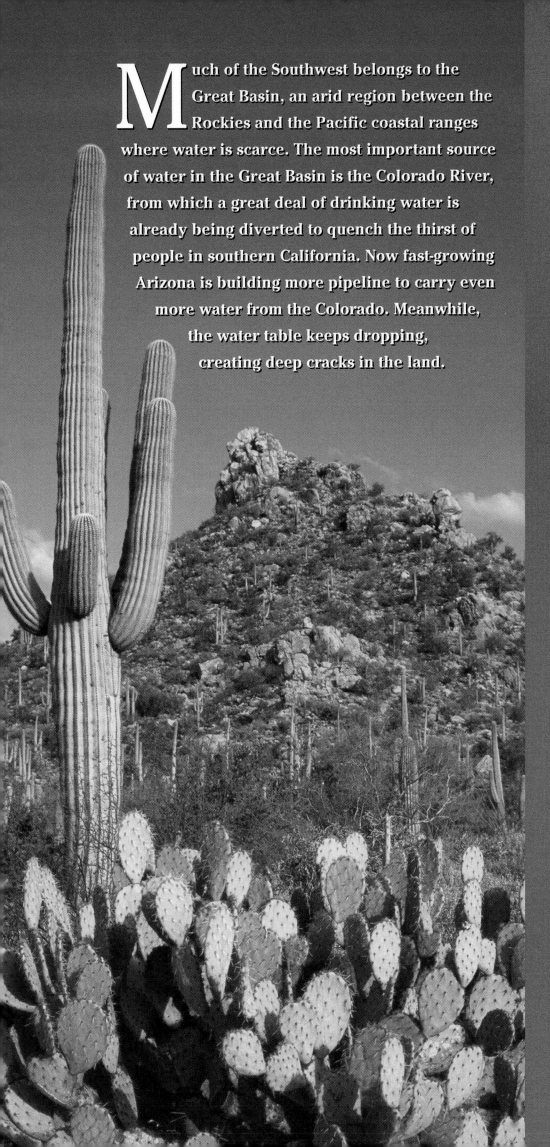

M uch of the Southwest belongs to the Great Basin, an arid region between the Rockies and the Pacific coastal ranges where water is scarce. The most important source of water in the Great Basin is the Colorado River, from which a great deal of drinking water is already being diverted to quench the thirst of people in southern California. Now fast-growing Arizona is building more pipeline to carry even more water from the Colorado. Meanwhile, the water table keeps dropping, creating deep cracks in the land.

Southwest

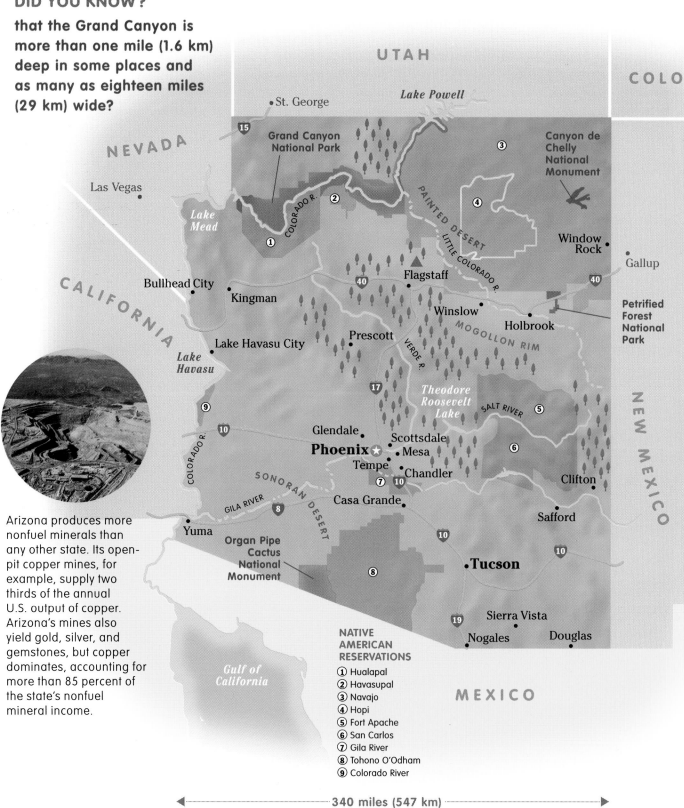

LEGEND

🛡20 Interstate Highways	⭐ State Capital	▫ Native American Reservations	🌲 National Forests	▪ National Parks and Refuges	▲ Highest Point		miles 0 — 100 kilometers 0 — 161

DID YOU KNOW?

that the Grand Canyon is more than one mile (1.6 km) deep in some places and as many as eighteen miles (29 km) wide?

UTAH

COLO

NEVADA

Lake Powell

• St. George

🛡15

Grand Canyon National Park

Canyon de Chelly National Monument

③

• Las Vegas

Lake Mead

COLORADO R.

🛡2

PAINTED DESERT

④

Window Rock

• Gallup

Bullhead City

🛡40

Flagstaff

LITTLE COLORADO R.

CALIFORNIA

Kingman

Winslow

Holbrook

🛡40

Petrified Forest National Park

MOGOLLON RIM

Prescott

Lake Havasu City

Lake Havasu

VERDE R.

🛡17

Theodore Roosevelt Lake

SALT RIVER

⑤

🛡9

Glendale

Scottsdale

⑥

NEW MEXICO

🛡10

Phoenix ⭐

Mesa

COLORADO R.

Tempe

Chandler

Clifton

SONORAN DESERT

🛡7

🛡10

Casa Grande

GILA RIVER

🛡8

Safford

Yuma

Organ Pipe Cactus National Monument

🛡10

🛡10

⑧

• Tucson

Sierra Vista

🛡19

Gulf of California

Nogales

Douglas

MEXICO

NATIVE AMERICAN RESERVATIONS

① Hualapal
② Havasupal
③ Navajo
④ Hopi
⑤ Fort Apache
⑥ San Carlos
⑦ Gila River
⑧ Tohono O'Odham
⑨ Colorado River

← 340 miles (547 km) →

Arizona produces more nonfuel minerals than any other state. Its open-pit copper mines, for example, supply two thirds of the annual U.S. output of copper. Arizona's mines also yield gold, silver, and gemstones, but copper dominates, accounting for more than 85 percent of the state's nonfuel mineral income.

ABOUT ARIZONA

NICKNAME: Grand Canyon State

CAPITAL: Phoenix

STATEHOOD: February 14, 1912 (48th)

MOTTO: God enriches.

POPULATION: 4,778,332 (20th)

AREA: 114,006 sq. mi. (6th)
(295,148 sq km)

HIGHEST POINT: 12,633 ft. (Humphreys Peak)

LOWEST POINT: 70 ft. (Colorado River)

FLOWER: Saguaro

TREE: Paloverde

BIRD: Cactus wren

FISH: Apache trout

Arizona

Until the 1960s, life in the Arizona desert appealed mostly to people with breathing problems. Then with the advent of affordable air-conditioning, retired Americans also began to take advantage of the region's clean air and sunshine. Today, people of all ages are flocking to Arizona, which trails only Nevada as the fastest-growing state. These newcomers are part of a larger national shift away from the northeastern Rust Belt, where manufacturing jobs have dwindled, to the booming economies of the Sun Belt.

Despite Arizona's many wide-open spaces, most newcomers have settled in the sprawling suburbs of Phoenix and Tucson, where three out of four Arizonans live. Sadly, this flood of people has threatened the very qualities of life that once made the state attractive. All these people drive cars that pollute the air, live in developments that block the scenery, and generally strain Arizona's resources, especially its water.

Arizona's most important source of water is the Colorado River, running through the 277-mile-long (446-kilometer-long) Grand Canyon. The canyon sits on the western edge of the scenic Colorado Plateau, a dry, high tableland cut by deep gorges and studded with mesas. A line of cliffs called the Mogollon Rim separates the Colorado Plateau from the Basin

Although no longer a part of Mexico, Arizona continues to maintain strong ties to its southern neighbor. Because one in five Arizonans is Hispanic, Mexican influences abound. Mexican architecture, home furnishings, clothing, music, and food have all become important parts of the Arizona lifestyle.

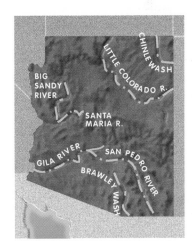

Mapmakers use dots and dashes to show rivers that dry up during part of the year. There are many such intermittent rivers in Arizona. Stretches of the Little Colorado, for example, flow only during winter and spring, when rains and melting snow provide sufficient water.

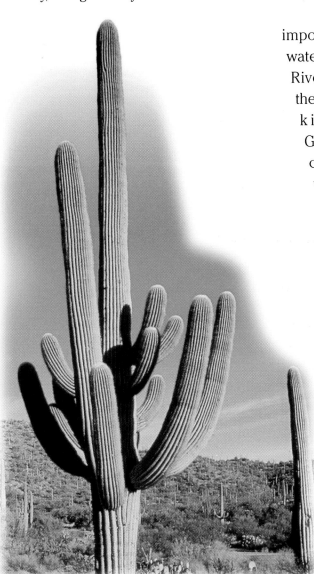

The Sonoran Desert contains many unique plants and animals. The most famous of these is the saguaro cactus, which can grow fifty feet (15 m) tall and live for more than one hundred years.

LEGEND

Interstate Highways	State Capital	Native American Reservations	National Forests	National Parks and Refuges	Highest Point	0 ... miles ... 100	
						0 ... kilometers ... 161	

DID YOU KNOW?

that Nevada, with no waiting periods and many drive-through chapels, leads the nation in weddings with ten times the national average?

OREGON

IDAHO

Duck Valley Reservation

BLACK ROCK DESERT

Winnemucca

HUMBOLDT RIVER

Elko

Pyramid Lake Reservation

Battle Mountain

RUBY MTS.

Pyramid Lake

TRUCKEE R.

CALIFORNIA

Reno

Sparks

Carson City

Walker River Reservation

SHOSHONE MOUNTAINS

Goshute Reservation

UTAH

Lake Tahoe

WALKER R.

Walker Lake

Ely

MONITOR RANGE

Hawthorne

Great Basin National Park

Tonopah

Death Valley National Monument

Groom Lake

Caliente

MEADOW VALLEY WASH

Gambling—along with hotels, restaurants, and other services that support it—employs more than half of the Nevada workforce. Overall, tourism contributes more to the economy than agriculture, mining, and manufacturing combined. Luxury casinos on the Las Vegas Strip allow visitors to spend fairy-tale nights in ancient Rome, Egypt, Paris, Venice, and New York City.

Las Vegas

Paradise

Henderson

Lake Mead

ARIZONA

COLORADO RIVER

◄———————— 320 miles (515 km) ————————►

ABOUT NEVADA

NICKNAME: Silver State

CAPITAL: Carson City

STATEHOOD: October 31, 1864 (36th)

MOTTO: All for our country.

POPULATION: 1,809,253 (35th)

AREA: 110,567 sq. mi. (7th) (286,245 sq km)

HIGHEST POINT: 13,140 ft. (Boundary Peak)

LOWEST POINT: 479 ft. (Colorado River)

FLOWER: Sagebrush

TREE: Single-leaf piñon, bristlecone pine

BIRD: Mountain bluebird

FISH: Lahontan cutthroat trout

Nevada

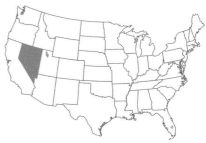

Because of its excessively dry climate and barren landscape, Nevada was one of the last U.S. territories to be explored and settled. Nineteenth-century gold and silver strikes lured prospectors—and Nevada still leads the nation in gold and silver mining—but those prospectors didn't stay long. During the Great Depression, Nevada attracted some attention with laws that made marriage and divorce much easier, yet it was legalized gambling, enacted in 1931, that assured the state's future prosperity.

Although Nevada retains many raucous frontier qualities, casino money has transformed both Las Vegas and Reno into sophisticated metropolitan areas housing more than 80 percent of the state's population. With the exception of the southern desert, the rest of the state belongs to what residents call the "cow counties," where cattle and sheep graze on leased public land before being shipped to California or the Midwest for fattening. The lack of water, of course, limits most other types of agriculture.

In fact, with just nine inches (23 cm) of precipitation per year, Nevada is the driest state. Except for a small spur of the Sierra Nevada near Lake Tahoe, most of Nevada belongs to the arid Great Basin. The water that makes Las Vegas possible comes primarily from Lake Mead, the largest U.S. reservoir, which stretches for 115 miles (185 km) behind Hoover Dam on the Colorado River.

Nevada's clear skies and open desert terrain provide ideal conditions for testing military aircraft. Over the years, many mysterious planes have been tested at Area 51, a top-secret air force base near Groom Lake. Often these planes are mistaken for UFOs. As a result, Route 375, which runs past Groom Lake, has been nick-named the Extraterrestrial Highway.

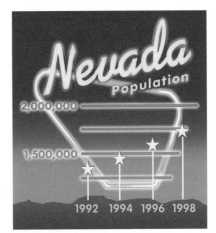

Nevada is the nation's fastest-growing state. Since 1980, its population has more than doubled. Nearly all that growth has come within existing metropolitan areas, especially the suburbs of Las Vegas.

Although Nevada averages nine inches (23 cm) of precipitation per year statewide, less than four inches (10 cm) of rain falls on the parched southern Nevada desert, where Death Valley National Monument is located.

LEGEND

🛣️ 20	✪	🟩	🌲	🟥	🔺	0 —— miles —— 100	
Interstate Highways	State Capital	Native American Reservations	National Forests	National Parks and Refuges	Highest Point	0 —— kilometers —— 161	

Since the 1940s, the Los Alamos National Laboratory has made New Mexico a center for scientific research. Los Alamos and other federal facilities, including the Sandia National Laboratories in Albuquerque, attract highly educated workers, often from outside the state.

UTAH · COLORADO · OKLA

Durango

① Farmington
SAN JUAN RIVER
②
㉒
Taos ③
Raton

DID YOU KNOW?

that at Four Corners on the Navajo Reservation you can lie down in four states at the same time?

④
⑤ ⑥ ⑦
⑧
Los Alamos
Gallup
RIO PUERCO
⑩ ⑨
⑩ ⑫
⑩ ⑪ ⑬
⑭
⑮
Rio Rancho
Santa Fe ⭐
Las Vegas
25
Conchas Lake
CANADIAN R.

40
Albuquerque 40
⑯
⑭
⑰ ⑭
⑭
Tucumcari

⑳ ⑲

⑱
Socorro
RIO GRANDE
25
GILA RIVER
PECOS RIVER
Clovis
Portales

Roswell

MAJOR NATIVE AMERICAN RESERVATIONS

① Ute Mountain
② Jicarilla Apache
③ Taos
④ Santa Clara
⑤ San Ildefonso
⑥ Pojoaque
⑦ Nambe
⑧ Tesuque
⑨ Jemez
⑩ Zia
⑪ Santa Ana
⑫ Santo Domingo
⑬ San Filipe
⑭ Laguna
⑮ Cañoncito
⑯ Isleta
⑰ Acoma
⑱ Alamo Navajo
⑲ Ramah Navajo
⑳ Zuni
㉑ Mescalero
㉒ Navajo

Elephant Butte Reservoir
Truth or Consequences
㉑
Alamogordo
Hobbs
Carlsbad

Silver City
Las Cruces
White Sands National Monument
Carlsbad Caverns National Park

10
Deming
10
El Paso

ARIZONA · MEXICO · TEXAS

◄——————— 352 miles (566 km) ———————►

ABOUT NEW MEXICO

NICKNAME: Land of Enchantment
CAPITAL: Santa Fe
STATEHOOD: January 6, 1912 (47th)
MOTTO: It grows as it goes.

POPULATION: 1,739,844 (37th)
AREA: 121,598 sq. mi. (5th)
(314,803 sq km)
HIGHEST POINT: 13,161 ft. (Wheeler Peak)
LOWEST POINT: 2,842 ft. (Red Bluff Reservoir)

FLOWER: Yucca
TREE: Piñon
BIRD: Roadrunner
FISH: Rio Grande cutthroat trout

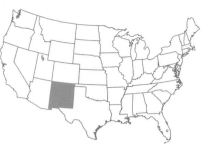

NAME GIVEN BY SIXTEENTH-CENTURY SPANIARDS TO THE LAND NORTH AND WEST OF THE RIO GRANDE.

New Mexico

For many years, New Mexico has attracted top artists from all over the world. Painters, notably Georgia O'Keeffe, came to record the state's unique physical beauty. Writers, on the other hand, have generally been more interested in observing New Mexico's extraordinary cultural diversity. With a population that's 40 percent Hispanic (the highest percentage of any state) and 9 percent Native American (the second highest percentage), New Mexico is an ongoing experiment. The purpose of this experiment? To find out how people of radically different backgrounds can live together while still maintaining their separate cultural identities.

Although art galleries have prospered in Santa Fe and Taos, most New Mexicans depend on farming, ranching, and mining for their livelihoods. New Mexico, for example, ranks third in copper production, sixth in uranium, and enjoys large reserves of oil, coal, and natural gas. In 1999, despite some local opposition, the nation's first permanent nuclear waste disposal site opened in the desert east of Carlsbad, accepting radioactive waste from Los Alamos and other nuclear weapons laboratories.

New Mexico's eastern third, a part of the Great Plains, is often called Little Texas because its cattle ranches, oil fields, and military bases remind people of the state next door. Farther west, the fertile Rio Grande Valley runs through the southern Rockies. The rest of the state belongs to the high Colorado Plateau in the northwest and a Basin and Range system in the south.

The Navajo of New Mexico are famous for their blankets, the Zuni for their turquoise-and-silver jewelry, and the Pueblo for their pots. Pueblo pottery is typically painted with geometric designs that identify the potter's village.

Humorist Will Rogers once called the enormous Carlsbad Caverns "the Grand Canyon with a roof on it." From late spring through fall, three hundred thousand Mexican free-tailed bats depart nightly at dusk to hunt for insects. People have compared this swarm with a column of smoke rising from the cave entrance.

From the desert basins of southern New Mexico, the land rises steadily as one moves north, climbing ten thousand feet (3,000 m) to the snowy Sangre de Cristo Mountains north of Taos.

LEGEND

 Interstate Highways

 State Capital

Native American Reservations

National Forests

National Parks and Refuges

Grasslands

▲ Highest Point

| 0 | miles | 100 |
| 0 | kilometers | 161 |

Pump It Up
Wells are a familiar sight in Oklahoma. In fact, eighteen wells once pumped oil from beneath the grounds of the state capitol. Although nearly every county in Oklahoma has oil and natural gas, the most important fields are found near Tulsa, the center of the state's petroleum industry.

DID YOU KNOW?
that Oklahoma averages fifty tornadoes a year, with the most coming in April and May?

KANSAS

COL.
N.M.

MISSOURI

ARKANSAS

TEXAS

Wichita

Salt Plains National Wildlife Refuge

Osage Reservation

SALT FORK RIVER

Alva

Great Salt Plains Lake

Ponca City

Bartlesville

Miami

Guymon

Optima Lake

Woodward

Enid

CIMARRON RIVER

Stillwater

Lake of the Cherokees

Tulsa

Canton Lake

CANADIAN R.

35

Broken Arrow

Edmond

Midwest City

44

Muskogee

ARKANSAS R.

Fort Smith

40

Elk City

Oklahoma City

Shawnee

40

Eufaula Lake

Robert S. Kerr Lake

Anadarko

Norman

WICHITA MTS.

WASHITA RIVER

Ada

McAlester

OUACHITA MTS.

Altus

Lawton

35

Broken Bow Lake

44

Duncan

Ardmore

Lake Texoma

Idabel

RED RIVER

Fort Worth   Dallas

← 464 miles (747 km) →

ABOUT OKLAHOMA

NICKNAME: Sooner State
CAPITAL: Oklahoma City
STATEHOOD: November 16, 1907 (46th)
MOTTO: Labor conquers all.

POPULATION: 3,358,044 (27th)
AREA: 69,903 sq. mi. (20th)
(180,971 sq km)
HIGHEST POINT: 4,973 ft. (Black Mesa)
LOWEST POINT: 289 ft. (Little River)

FLOWER: Mistletoe
TREE: Redbud
BIRD: Scissor-tailed flycatcher
FISH: White bass

Oklahoma

The people who live along the Red River in southern Oklahoma call their region Little Dixie because it reminds them of the Deep South, where their great-great-grandfathers farmed before moving west. Similarly, the wheat fields of northern Oklahoma show the influence of the transplanted Kansans who first tilled the soil there. However, from the Ouachita Mountains to the Panhandle, the rest of Oklahoma is truly cowboy country, and the state prides itself on its colorful western heritage.

For a long time, both the cowboys and the Native Americans in Oklahoma struggled. During the nineteenth century, Oklahoma was called the Indian Territory because the federal government had relocated so many Native Americans there. The terrain was so barren that no one thought whites would ever want to live there. Even during the twentieth century, the prolonged drought of the Dust Bowl years forced hundreds of thousands of Oklahomans to leave the state.

Yet today the descendants of Oklahoma's cowboys and Native Americans are flourishing. Improved soil conservation has reclaimed so much farmland that Oklahoma currently ranks fourth in wheat production. It also ranks third in beef cattle, the state's leading agricultural product. Even bigger money comes from oil and natural gas.

Overall, Oklahoma is a jumble of environments: The northeastern corner, for example, sits on the edge of the hilly, cool Ozark Plateau. The High Plains climate on the Panhandle, however, is much hotter and drier.

After California, Oklahoma has more Native American residents than any other state—about 260,000, or 7.8 percent of the population. Yet there are few reservations in Oklahoma because the Cherokee and other Native American nations have become so well integrated. In 1985, for example, the Cherokee Nation took the nontraditional step of electing its first female chief, Wilma Mankiller (pictured above).

Oklahoma has extremely varied microclimates because it occupies two weather transition zones: from north to south as well as from east to west. At any given time, cool northern, warm southern, dry western, or humid eastern air may dominate. However, when two or more of these air masses meet, the result can be blizzards, thunderstorms, and even tornadoes.

The humid Red River Valley defines Oklahoma's southern border with Texas. The farmers there grow cotton, peanuts, and other crops that immigrants from the South brought with them during the nineteenth century.

LEGEND

  Interstate Highways | ★ State Capital | ■ National Parks and Refuges | National Forests | Marshes | Grasslands | ▲ Highest Point

| 0 | miles | 100 |
| 0 | kilometers | 161 |

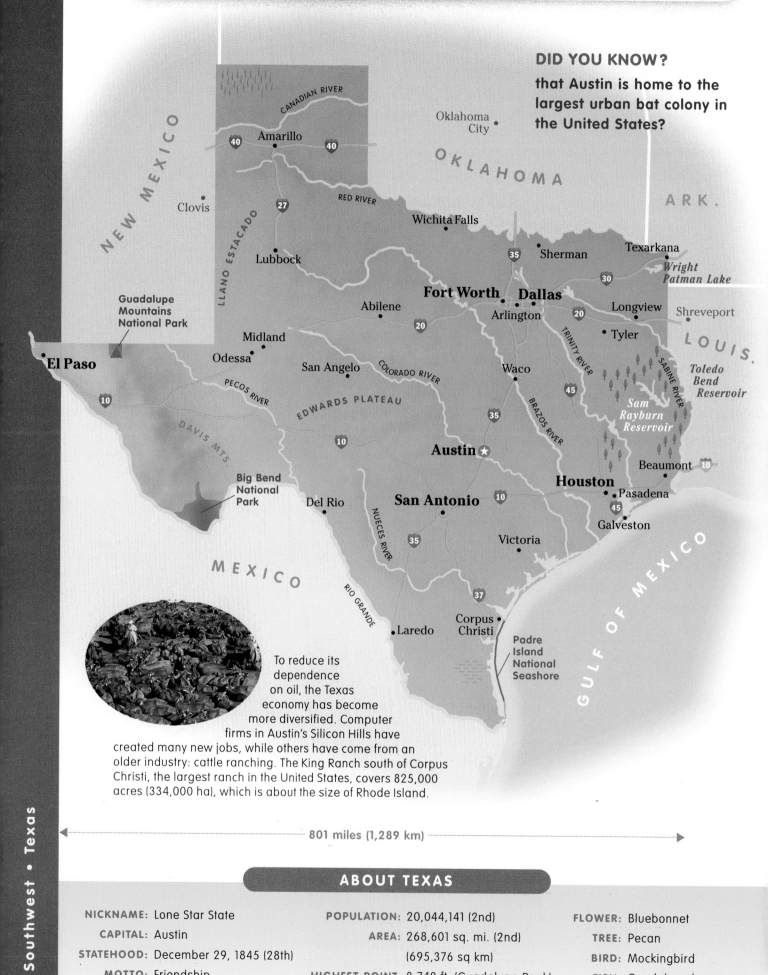

DID YOU KNOW?

that Austin is home to the largest urban bat colony in the United States?

NEW MEXICO

CANADIAN RIVER

Amarillo

Clovis

LLANO ESTACADO

Lubbock

RED RIVER

Guadalupe Mountains National Park

El Paso

PECOS RIVER

Odessa

Midland

San Angelo

COLORADO RIVER

EDWARDS PLATEAU

DAVIS MTS.

Big Bend National Park

Del Rio

NUECES RIVER

MEXICO

RIO GRANDE

Laredo

Abilene

Fort Worth

Arlington

Waco

Austin ★

San Antonio

Victoria

Corpus Christi

OKLAHOMA

Oklahoma City

Wichita Falls

Sherman

Dallas

ARK.

Texarkana

Wright Patman Lake

Longview   Shreveport

Tyler

LOUIS.

TRINITY RIVER

SABINE RIVER

Toledo Bend Reservoir

Sam Rayburn Reservoir

BRAZOS RIVER

Houston

Beaumont

Pasadena

Galveston

Padre Island National Seashore

GULF OF MEXICO

To reduce its dependence on oil, the Texas economy has become more diversified. Computer firms in Austin's Silicon Hills have created many new jobs, while others have come from an older industry: cattle ranching. The King Ranch south of Corpus Christi, the largest ranch in the United States, covers 825,000 acres (334,000 ha), which is about the size of Rhode Island.

◄———————— 801 miles (1,289 km) ————————►

ABOUT TEXAS

NICKNAME: Lone Star State
CAPITAL: Austin
STATEHOOD: December 29, 1845 (28th)
MOTTO: Friendship.

POPULATION: 20,044,141 (2nd)
AREA: 268,601 sq. mi. (2nd)
(695,376 sq km)
HIGHEST POINT: 8,749 ft. (Guadalupe Peak)
LOWEST POINT: Sea level (Gulf of Mexico)

FLOWER: Bluebonnet
TREE: Pecan
BIRD: Mockingbird
FISH: Guadalupe bass

Texas

When Texas joined the Union in 1845, Congress gave it the right to divide itself into five states of more manageable size. Instead, Texas has remained huge—the second largest state, the second most populous, and among the wealthiest. Over the years, Texans have used their valuable natural resources, particularly oil, to fund the growth of profitable manufacturing industries, such as chemical production.

Houston, the center of the U.S. petroleum industry and one of the nation's busiest ports, sits on the Gulf Coastal Plain, which covers the state's eastern third. This highly industrialized and densely populated region includes Texas's best farmland and its most productive oil fields.

A line drawn from Fort Worth to San Antonio would separate the moist coastal plain from the dry, treeless hill country, where cattle ranching still dominates. Ranching is also the dominant industry on the High Plains of the Panhandle—where, it's said, the cowboy spirit endures. Farther south, in the Rio Grande Valley, an eleven-month growing season allows farmers to raise winter vegetables and some citrus fruit.

The Rio Grande Valley is also known for its high concentration of Mexican Americans. Hispanics account for more than a quarter of Texas's population, making them an important political force in cities such as El Paso and San Antonio. In fact, census projections suggest that Texas will one day have a Hispanic majority.

Austin calls itself the Live Music Capital of the World because of the many clubs lining downtown Sixth Street. The diverse styles heard there include blues, country, jazz, swing, and Tejano.

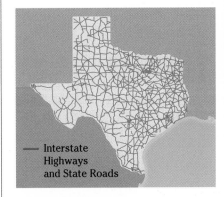

— Interstate Highways and State Roads

Texas has more streets and highways than any other state. Its 294,833 total miles (474,386 km) are nearly twice that of second-place California. The state's annual roadway maintenance budget, which doesn't include money spent by towns or counties, is more than eight hundred million dollars, and its construction budget is nearly two billion dollars.

Texas boasts more than five thousand species of wildflowers. Although bluebonnet, pink evening primrose, and Indian paintbrush grow statewide, most varieties are confined to a particular region.

113

ARCTIC OCEAN

RUSSIA

YUKON RIVER

Alaska
page 116

BERING SEA

CANADA

PACIFIC OCEAN

Washington
page 124

COLUMBIA R.

SNAKE R.

Oregon
page 122

Hawaii
page 120

California
page 118

MEXICO

The Coast Ranges of California, Oregon, and Washington form a line along which the Pacific and North American plates (part of the earth's crust) crunch past one another. Earthquakes, with which most Californians are familiar, are one symptom of this stress. Another is volcanic activity, such as the eruption of Mount St. Helens in 1980. The Aleutian Islands of Alaska also sit on this Ring of Fire, the name given to the edge of the Pacific Plate along which most of the earth's active volcanoes are located.

Pacific

LEGEND

⭐ State Capital   ■ National Parks and Refuges   ■ Tundra   ▲ Highest Point

0	miles	300
0	km	483

The Trans-Alaska Pipeline carries oil from Prudhoe Bay, where the coast is frozen eight months a year, to the ice-free port of Valdez eight hundred miles (1,300 km) away. Terrain permitting, the four-foot-wide (one-meter-wide) pipeline is buried. However, across the permanently frozen Arctic tundra, it's typically raised on supports that allow migrating caribou to pass underneath.

ARCTIC OCEAN
Barrow
Chukchi Sea
NORTH SLOPE
Prudhoe Bay
COLVILLE RIVER
BROOKS RANGE
NOATAK RIVER
Kotzebue
⑦
PORCUPINE R.
⑧
YUKON RIVER
RUSSIA
Bering Strait
Nome
KOYUKUK R.
CANADA
YUKON RIVER
KUSKOKWIM MTS.
College • Fairbanks
TANANA RIVER
BERING SEA
KUSKOKWIN RIVER
ALASKA RANGE
⑥
KUSKOKWIM RIVER
WRANGELL MTS.
Bethel
Anchorage
②
Whitehorse
⑤
Valdez
Kenai
Cordova
③
Prince William Sound
Skagway
ALEUTIAN RANGE
④
①
Kodiak
Juneau ☆
Gulf of Alaska
Sitka
Kodiak Island
Alexander Archipelago
Cold Bay
Ketchikan
Unalaska
Aleutian Islands
PACIFIC OCEAN

DID YOU KNOW?

that because the Matanuska Valley north of Anchorage gets twenty hours of sunlight during summer, cabbages there grow to nearly one hundred pounds (45 kg)?

NATIONAL PARKS
① Glacier Bay
② Wrangell–St. Elias
③ Kenai Fjords
④ Katmai
⑤ Lake Clark
⑥ Denali
⑦ Gates of the Arctic
⑧ Kobuk Valley

‹---- 2,400 miles (3,862 km) ----›

ABOUT ALASKA

NICKNAME: Last Frontier
CAPITAL: Juneau
STATEHOOD: January 3, 1959 (49th)
MOTTO: North to the future.

POPULATION: 619,500 (48th)
AREA: 656,424 sq. mi. (1st)
(1,699,404 sq km)
HIGHEST POINT: 20,320 ft. (Mount McKinley)
LOWEST POINT: Sea level (Pacific Ocean)

FLOWER: Forget-me-not
TREE: Sitka spruce
BIRD: Willow ptarmigan
FISH: King salmon

Alaska

Alaska can be a hard place to live because of the cold climate and rough terrain. In January, for example, the temperature in Fairbanks rarely rises above 0°F (-18°C), and even during the summer months, mountain ranges and ice fields make ground-level travel difficult, as do the great distances involved.

Alaskans have made up for this isolation by using satellite telephones and the Internet to connect to the outside world. Among the most ardent users of these new technologies are the native people who make up 16 percent of the population. Even so, many Aleuts and Inuit still live off the land, hunting and fishing as their ancestors did.

The dominant physical feature of the Alaskan Panhandle is the Inside Passage, a sheltered waterway stretching from Skagway to Seattle, Washington. Through its channels runs the Alaska Marine Highway, a state-operated ferry system that services towns with little or no road access. Far more remote are the fogbound Aleutian Islands, jutting eleven hundred miles (1,800 km) into the North Pacific.

Inland, north of the Alaska Range, sits the Yukon Plateau, beyond which few Alaskans live. From the crest of the little-explored Brooks Range, the land slopes down to the Arctic Coastal Plain, where immense oil fields were discovered in 1968. Currently, oil revenues fund about 85 percent of the state budget, but Alaskans have also had to live with oil's environmental consequences, such as the 1989 *Exxon Valdez* spill that polluted Prince William Sound.

In rugged Alaska, the family "car" is often a small airplane. One out of every fifty-eight Alaskans has a license to fly, which is six times the national average. Even where there are roads, snowmobiles often take the place of cars in winter.

Alaska, the largest state, accounts for one sixth of the nation's total area. If you superimposed a map of Alaska on a map of the continental United States, Alaska would stretch all the way from Savannah, Georgia, to Los Angeles and reach as far north as the Canadian border.

The towering peaks of the Alaska Range dominate the southern half of the state. These include Mount McKinley, the highest point in North America. Of the twenty tallest U.S. mountains, seventeen are in Alaska.

117

Interstate Highways · State Capital · Native American Reservations · National Forests · National Parks and Refuges · Highest Point

| 0 | miles | 100 |
| 0 | kilometers | 161 |

OREGON

Redwood National Park

KLAMATH RIVER

KLAMATH MTS.

CASCADE MTS.

Goose Lake

① Eureka

Shasta Lake

Lassen Volcanic National Park

EEL RIVER

Redding

② COAST RANGES

Chico

SACRAMENTO R.

Reno

Clear Lake

80

Lake Tahoe

SIERRA NEVADA

Santa Rosa

505 ★ Sacramento

Berkeley

80

5 Stockton

San Francisco ● Oakland

Modesto

Sunnyvale ● San Jose ● Merced

Santa Cruz

SAN JOAQUIN R.

Salinas

Monterey

SALINAS RIVER

COAST RANGES

Fresno

5 Sequoia National Park ③

San Luis Obispo

Santa Barbara

Los Angeles Pasadena

Anaheim

Long Beach Santa Ana

Channel Islands National Park

Channel Islands

Yosemite National Park

Mono Lake

Kings Canyon National Park

Death Valley National Park

Las Vegas

NEVADA

In California's fertile Central Valley, farmers grow more than 350 varieties of fruits and vegetables. When processed, these crops make up about 40 percent of the nation's canned and frozen produce. Supermarkets can sell California produce cheaply because much of it is picked by migrant workers who work under difficult conditions for little pay.

MAJOR NATIVE AMERICAN RESERVATIONS

① Hoopa Valley
② Round Valley
③ Tule River
④ Aqua Caliente

MOJAVE DESERT

15

Barstow

40 Joshua Tree National Park

15 San Bernardino

Riverside ④

10

Salton Sea

5 15

Escondido

San Diego

Chula Vista

Tijuana

ARIZONA

COLORADO RIVER

MEXICO

PACIFIC OCEAN

DID YOU KNOW?

that the highest (Mount Whitney) and the lowest (Death Valley) points in the continental United States are only sixty miles (97 km) apart?

← 350 miles (563 km) →

ABOUT CALIFORNIA

NICKNAME: Golden State
CAPITAL: Sacramento
STATEHOOD: September 9, 1850 (31st)
MOTTO: Eureka!

POPULATION: 33,145,121 (1st)
AREA: 163,707 sq. mi. (3rd)
(423,818 sq km)
HIGHEST POINT: 14,494 ft. (Mount Whitney)
LOWEST POINT: -282 ft. (Death Valley)

FLOWER: Golden poppy
TREE: California redwood
BIRD: California valley quail
FISH: California golden trout

California

CALIFORNIA REPUBLIC

A century ago, immigrants from all over the world flocked to New York City to earn their fortunes. Since World War II, however, even New Yorkers have gone to California to make their dreams come true—and not just out-of-work actors. Today, it's impossible to overstate California's economic, political, and cultural importance. The state ranks first in both manufactured goods and farm income, and without California's votes it's difficult to win a presidential election. Cultural trends, too, now move from west to east: Two recent examples are organic foods and eastern religion (no doubt influenced by the many Asian Americans living in California). Overall, nearly one in eight Americans is a Californian, including half of all Mexican Americans and two fifths of all Asian Americans, many of whom are recent immigrants.

Although southern California is famous for its beaches, most of it sits on the Mojave Desert. As a result, the region has 50 percent of the state's population but only 2 percent of its water. That's why a complex system of dams and aqueducts has been built to divert water from elsewhere, principally the Colorado River.

North of the fertile Central Valley, which runs between the Coast Ranges and the Sierra Nevada, the Klamath and Cascade mountains rise above dense stands of timber. Except in the desert south, California has two seasons: a dry one from spring to fall and a rainy one the rest of the year.

Alice Waters, the founder of Berkeley's Chez Panisse restaurant, began a trend in cooking that has since come to be known as California cuisine. Her cooking emphasizes the freshest ingredients, usually grown organically on small local farms, and borrows freely from California's many immigrant cuisines, especially Asian and Mexican.

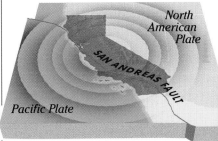

North American Plate

SAN ANDREAS FAULT

Pacific Plate

In earthquake-prone California, two of the plates that make up the earth's crust come together. The line along which they meet is called the San Andreas Fault. As the Pacific Plate creeps northwestward, it pushes against the North American Plate, causing pressure to build. From time to time, this pressure is released as an earthquake.

California's largest cities are all located at gaps in the Coast Ranges. Elsewhere, these mountains rise so abruptly from the Pacific that towns have no room to grow. There's barely enough room for State Route 1, which is often closed by mud slides.

LEGEND

★ State Capital

■ National Parks and Refuges

▲ Highest Point

| 0 | miles | 100 |
| 0 | kilometers | 161 |

DID YOU KNOW?

that despite the tropical climate, snow falls on Hawaii's tallest mountains?

Kauai

Kapaa
Kekaha Lihue
• Puuwai

Niihau

Oahu

Pearl City Kaneohe
Waipahu• •Kailua

★ **Honolulu**

Pearl Harbor

Molokai
•Kaunakakai

Maui

Lanai City• Wailuku
• •Kahului
Kihei•

Lanai

Haleakala National Park

Kahoolawe

P A C I F I C   O C E A N

Waimea
•

Hawaii

Kailua-Kona• WAILUKU R. •Hilo

Captain• Cook

Ka Lae•

Hawaii Volcanoes National Park

Hawaii leads the nation in raising bananas, papayas, guavas, macadamia nuts, and coffee, as well as pineapples, the state's most famous crop. Each year, the pineapple harvest brings in about one hundred million dollars.

◄———————— 353 miles (568 km) ————————►

ABOUT HAWAII

NICKNAME: Aloha State

CAPITAL: Honolulu

STATEHOOD: August 21, 1959 (50th)

MOTTO: The life of the land is perpetuated in righteousness.

POPULATION: 1,185,497 (42nd)

AREA: 10,932 sq. mi. (43rd) (28,302 sq km)

HIGHEST POINT: 13,796 ft. (Mauna Kea)

LOWEST POINT: Sea level (Pacific Ocean)

FLOWER: Yellow hibiscus

TREE: Kukui (candlenut)

BIRD: Nene (Hawaiian goose)

Hawaii

The familiar Hawaiian islands are, in fact, the eastern end of a sixteen-hundred-mile (twenty-six-hundred-kilometer) chain stretching from the Big Island of Hawaii northwest to tiny Kure Atoll. Nearly all Hawaiians live on the eight major islands, which are the cone-shaped tops of gigantic ocean volcanoes. Of these people, 21 percent are descendants of the Polynesians who originally settled Hawaii. The rest are 33 percent white, 20 percent Japanese, 10 percent Filipino, 3 percent Chinese, and 3 percent black, giving Hawaii the most diverse ethnic mix of any state.

Even so, Hawaii's population is dwarfed each year by the seven million tourists who bring with them ten billion dollars, by far the state's largest source of income. The next largest revenue producer is the federal government. Military bases such as Pearl Harbor house so many soldiers and sailors that military personnel and their families make up nearly one tenth of the state's population.

The most crowded island is Oahu, where about three in four Hawaiians live. The largest island is agricultural Hawaii. Kauai's lush valleys, Maui's wide beaches, and Lanai's seclusion are particularly popular with tourists, while Molokai and Niihau have especially high concentrations of native Hawaiians. On the tiny, privately owned island of Niihau, several hundred pure-blood Hawaiians raise livestock, speak their traditional language, and otherwise struggle to keep native traditions alive. Public access to Niihau is strictly limited, and no one at all is allowed on Kahoolawe, which until recently was a bombing range.

"Shaka, Brah"
Among young people in Hawaii, the "shaka" sign is the universal greeting. Given with the thumb pointing up and the pinkie pointing out, it means both "hello" and "peace"—and, more generally, "good vibes." It's often accompanied by the phrase "Shaka, Brah." (*Brah* is pidgin English for "brother.")

Mauna Kea

Mount Everest

33,476 ft
(10,203 m)

29,035 ft
(8,850 m)

The state's highest point, Mauna Kea on the Big Island of Hawaii, rises 13,796 feet (4,205 m) above sea level. It also extends nearly 20,000 feet (6,000 m) down to the bottom of the Hawaiian Trough. If you count this submerged base, Mauna Kea becomes the tallest mountain in the world, topping even Mount Everest.

The white sand that covers most Hawaiian beaches is made of tiny shell and coral fragments pulverized by the pounding surf. Some beaches, however, have black sand made of crushed obsidian, which is also called volcanic glass.

LEGEND

Interstate Highways	State Capital	Native American Reservations	National Forests	National Parks and Refuges	Highest Point		miles	kilometers	
20	★				▲	0	100		
						0	161		

Although the timber industry no longer dominates the state economy, it remains important to the way that Oregonians view themselves. Each July, for example, the Albany Timber Carnival sponsors popular competitions in log chopping, sawing, ax throwing, and birling (log rolling in water).

WASHINGTON

Astoria

Kennewick

82

COLUMBIA RIVER

Portland
Vancouver
The Dalles
84
Pendleton
Umatilla Reservation

Beaverton
Gresham
McMinnville

5

La Grande
84

BLUE MOUNTAINS

Salem
Albany

Warm Springs Reservation

JOHN DAY R.

Baker City

Corvallis

5

SNAKE RIVER

DESCHUTES R.

WILLAMETTE R.

Eugene
Springfield
Bend

Canyon City

Ontario

IDAHO

Boise

UMPQUA RIVER

HARNEY BASIN

Coos Bay

COAST RANGES

CASCADE RANGE

Malheur Lake

Roseburg

Crater Lake National Park

Harney Lake

STEENS MOUNTAINS

OWYHEE RIVER

ROGUE RIVER

Summer Lake

Lake Abert

ALVORD DESERT

Grants Pass

Upper Klamath Lake

Medford
Ashland
Klamath Falls
Altamont

Goose Lake

KLAMATH RIVER

PACIFIC OCEAN

NEVADA

CALIFORNIA

DID YOU KNOW?

that Oregon, a national leader in ecological legislation, passed the nation's first bottle-return law in 1971?

◄—————— 395 miles (636 km) ——————►

ABOUT OREGON

NICKNAME: Beaver State

CAPITAL: Salem

STATEHOOD: February 14, 1859 (33rd)

MOTTO: She flies with her own wings.

POPULATION: 3,316,154 (28th)

AREA: 98,386 sq. mi. (9th)
(254,710 sq km)

HIGHEST POINT: 11,239 ft. (Mount Hood)

LOWEST POINT: Sea level (Pacific Ocean)

FLOWER: Oregon grape

TREE: Douglas fir

BIRD: Western meadowlark

FISH: Chinook salmon

Pacific • Oregon

122

Oregon

STATE OF OREGON
1859

No one doubts that Oregonians love the outdoors. Excluding the state's passion for wrestling, bicycling and long-distance running are its most high-profile sports. Yet Oregon is also the nation's leading timber state, and until recently most Oregonians worked for timber-related companies. During the 1990s, though, they had to make hard choices between their jobs and the environment.

Some choices were made for them. To protect the habitat of the endangered northern spotted owl, the federal government severely restricted logging in public forests, which contain about half of Oregon's timber. In response, the state reduced its dependence on forestry by promoting high-tech industries like those in neighboring Washington and California.

Recent immigrants to Oregon say that they value the state's high quality of life, particularly its clean air and water, outdoor lifestyle, and many open spaces. In fact, outside the Willamette River Valley, Oregon is quite sparsely settled. The rainy, foggy, populated Oregon that most people picture in their minds exists only west of the Cascades. The rest of the state sits mostly on the dry, barren Columbia Plateau. Geologists call the land south of the Blue Mountains the High Lava Plains because it was once covered with lava from the volcano that erupted to form Crater Lake. To most people, though, this Utah-like landscape is simply the Oregon Desert.

Bicycle-friendly Portland has recently become even more so. In 1994, a community-based environmental group interested in reducing auto pollution began leaving free bicycles around the city for anyone to use. Riders are merely asked to return the bikes, painted a distinctive yellow, to a main street after each trip.

−1,932 ft.

Nearly eight thousand years ago, a volcano erupted in southern Oregon. The explosion blew off the mountain's peak, leaving behind a crater that has since filled with rainwater and snowmelt. Intensely blue Crater Lake is, at 1,932 feet (589 m), the deepest lake in the United States and the seventh deepest in the world.

Most Oregonians live in the fertile Willamette River Valley, running south from the Columbia River between the Coast Range and the Cascades. Many farms there grow flowering bulbs and plants such as tulips and the irises pictured at left.

Interstate Highways

State Capital

Native American Reservations

National Forests

National Parks and Refuges

Highest Point

| 0 | | miles | | 100 |
| 0 | | kilometers | | 161 |

CANADA

DID YOU KNOW?

that the San Juan Islands in Puget Sound increase from 428 to 743 islands between high and low tides?

Vancouver

Point Roberts

North Cascades National Park

Bellingham

San Juan Islands

Strait of San Juan de Fuca

Puget Sound

Colville Reservation

KETTLE RIVER RANGE

COLUMBIA RIVER

SKAGIT RIVER

Everett

CASCADE RANGE

Lake Chelan

WENATCHEE MTS.

Banks Lake

Grand Coulee

SPOKANE RIVER

Spokane Reservation

Port Angeles

OLYMPIC MTS.

Seattle

Bellevue

Federal Way

Tacoma

90

Wenatchee

Ephrata

Moses Lake

Spokane

IDAHO

Olympic National Park

COAST RANGES

Quinault Reservation

Aberdeen

Olympia

Mount Rainier National Park

Ellensburg

Potholes Reservoir

90

Centralia

Yakima

COLUMBIA RIVER

SNAKE RIVER

PACIFIC OCEAN

Longview Kelso

5

Mt. St. Helens National Volcanic Monument

Vancouver

Richland

YAKIMA RIVER

Kennewick

Walla Walla

82

Yakima Reservation

Portland

OREGON

Dams on the Snake and Columbia rivers produce about one third of all U.S. hydroelectric power. The most impressive is the Grand Coulee Dam, the nation's largest concrete structure. Many Washington businesses depend on its cheap renewable energy, such as the Reynolds Metals aluminum-smelting plant in Longview.

◀——————— 360 miles (579 km) ———————▶

ABOUT WASHINGTON

NICKNAME: Evergreen State

CAPITAL: Olympia

STATEHOOD: November 11, 1889 (42nd)

MOTTO: By and by.

POPULATION: 5,756,361 (15th)

AREA: 71,302 sq. mi. (18th)

(184,592 sq km)

HIGHEST POINT: 14,410 ft. (Mount Rainier)

LOWEST POINT: Sea level (Pacific Ocean)

FLOWER: Coast rhododendron

TREE: Western hemlock

BIRD: Willow goldfinch

FISH: Steelhead trout

Washington

Besides the rain, what's not to like about Washington? From the snowcapped mountains to the islands of Puget Sound, the scenery is spectacular, and the state's economy is equally breathtaking. Perhaps that's why Seattle has become one of the nation's most desirable and fastest-growing cities.

About two thirds of the state's population lives on the shores of Puget Sound, where shipbuilding used to be the leading industry. Now it's computers. Boasting more than two thousand software companies, notably Microsoft, the Puget Sound basin has come to rival California's Silicon Valley as the nation's leading high-tech, high-wage center.

Elsewhere in western Washington, forestry companies harvest the abundant timber growing on the western slopes of the Olympic and Cascade mountains. That's where most of the rain falls, as much as two hundred inches (500 cm) per year. All that moisture nourishes a unique temperate rain forest thickly carpeted with ferns and mosses.

Yet just a few miles over the Cascades in eastern Washington, the Columbia Plateau is so dry that dams are needed to irrigate the fields. With enough water, though, the rich volcanic soil of the Columbia Plateau is well suited to agriculture. Among the most valuable crops grown there are apples, cherries, asparagus, raspberries, and wine grapes. The warm days, cool nights, and sandy soil of the Columbia River basin resemble the vineyard conditions in France, making for excellent grape growing.

As well as skiing, sailing, and mountain climbing, Washington-ians are particularly fond of wildlife watching. The ferry that carries commuters from the San Juan Islands to Seattle also provides the occasional opportunity to view the orcas, minke whales, and seals that live in Puget Sound.

Why is western Washington so wet and eastern Washington so dry? Because the height of the Cascades forces clouds to drop their moisture before passing over. That's why the Olympic Peninsula receives 125 inches (318 cm) of precipitation per year and Richland on the Columbia River only 7 inches (18 cm).

Most of the high peaks in the Cascades are dormant volcanoes, yet every so often one becomes active. On May 18, 1980, long-dormant Mount St. Helens erupted, blanketing most of the Northwest with volcanic ash.

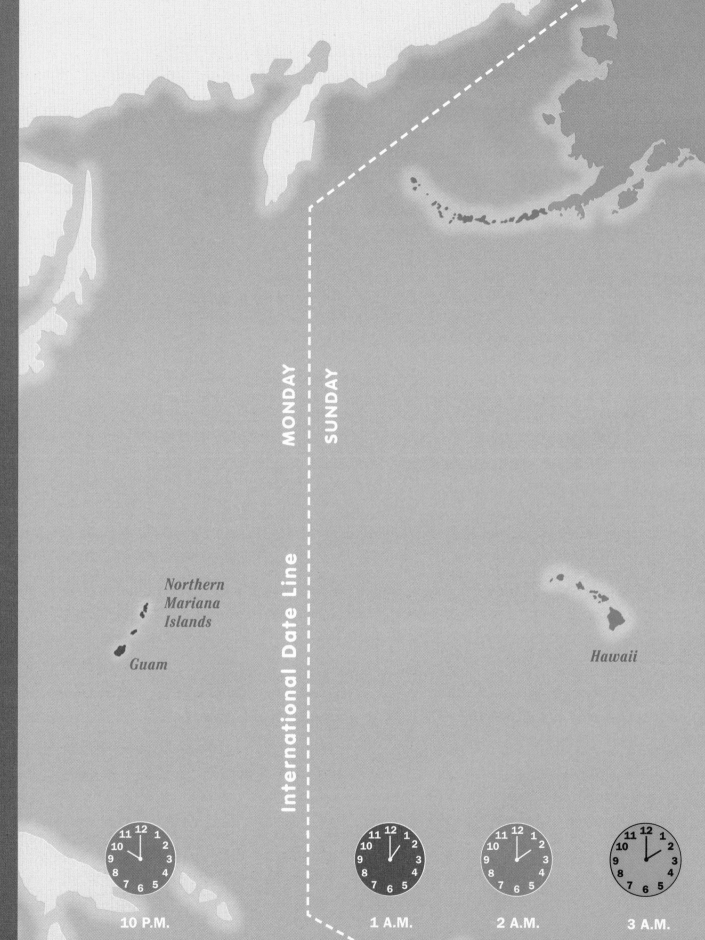

Northern
Mariana
Islands

Guam

International Date Line

MONDAY

SUNDAY

Hawaii

10 P.M.

1 A.M.

2 A.M.

3 A.M.

American Samoa

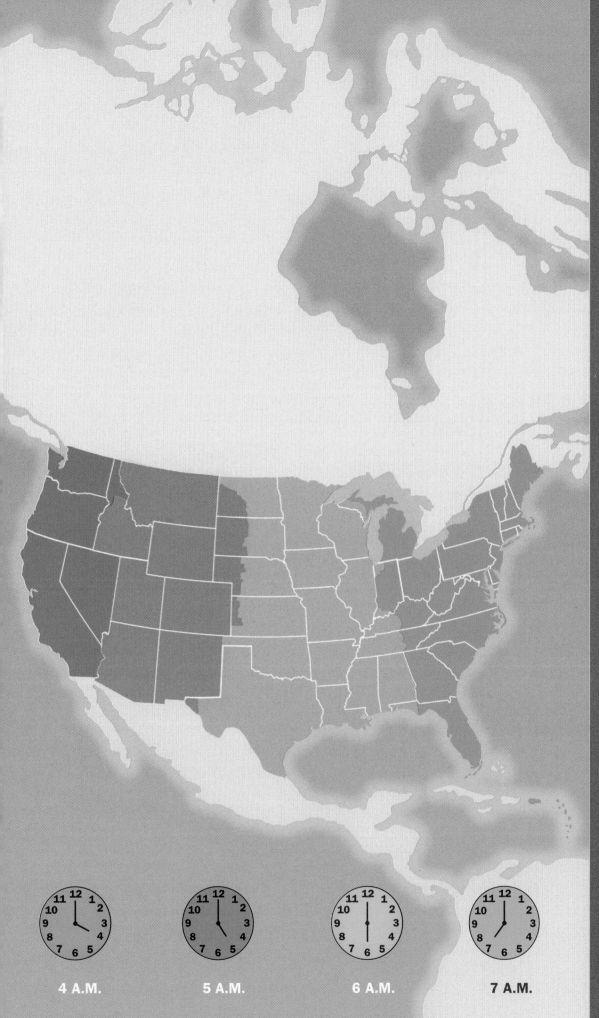

4 A.M.　　　　5 A.M.　　　　6 A.M.　　　　7 A.M.

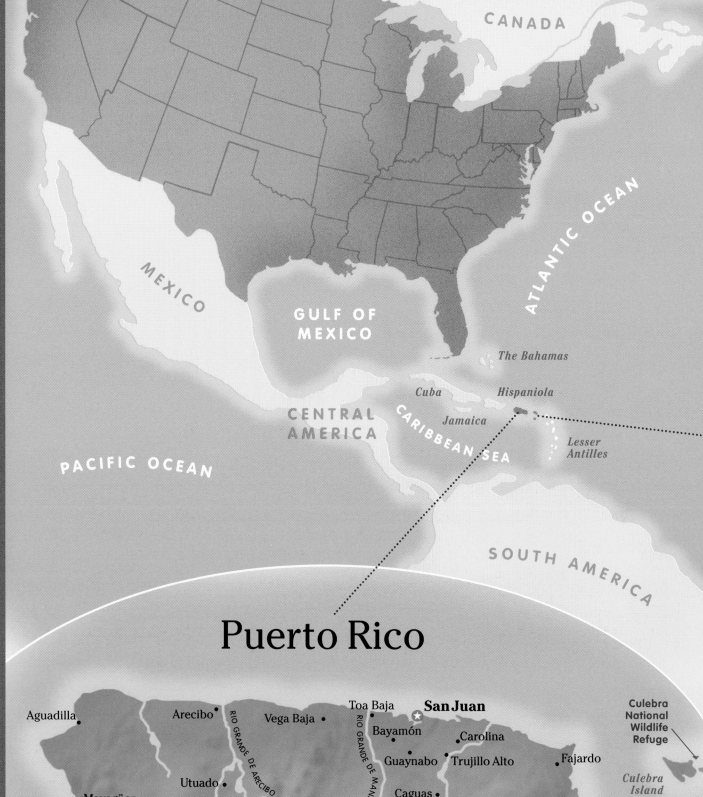

CANADA

ATLANTIC OCEAN

MEXICO

GULF OF
MEXICO

The Bahamas

Cuba

Hispaniola

CENTRAL
AMERICA

CARIBBEAN SEA

Jamaica

*Lesser
Antilles*

PACIFIC OCEAN

SOUTH AMERICA

Puerto Rico

Aguadilla

Arecibo

Vega Baja

RIO GRANDE DE ARECIBO

Toa Baja

San Juan

Bayamón

RIO GRANDE DE MANATI

Carolina

Culebra
National
Wildlife
Refuge

Guaynabo

Trujillo Alto

Fajardo

Utuado

*Culebra
Island*

Mayagüez

Caguas

Cabo Rojo
National
Wildlife
Refuge

San Germán

Humacao

Isabel
Segunda

Cayey

CORDILLERA CENTRAL

Ponce

SIERRA DE CAYEY

Vieques Island

Guayama

Laguna Cartagena
National Wildlife
Refuge

112 miles (180 km)

Atlantic Possessions

St. Thomas

★ **Charlotte
Amalie**

St. John

Virgin
Islands
National
Park

U.S. Virgin
Islands

◄───────── **35 miles (56 km)** ─────────►

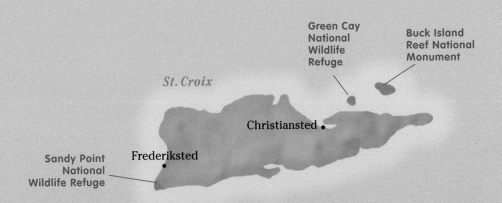

Green Cay
National
Wildlife
Refuge

Buck Island
Reef National
Monument

St. Croix

Christiansted •

Sandy Point
National
Wildlife Refuge

Frederiksted •

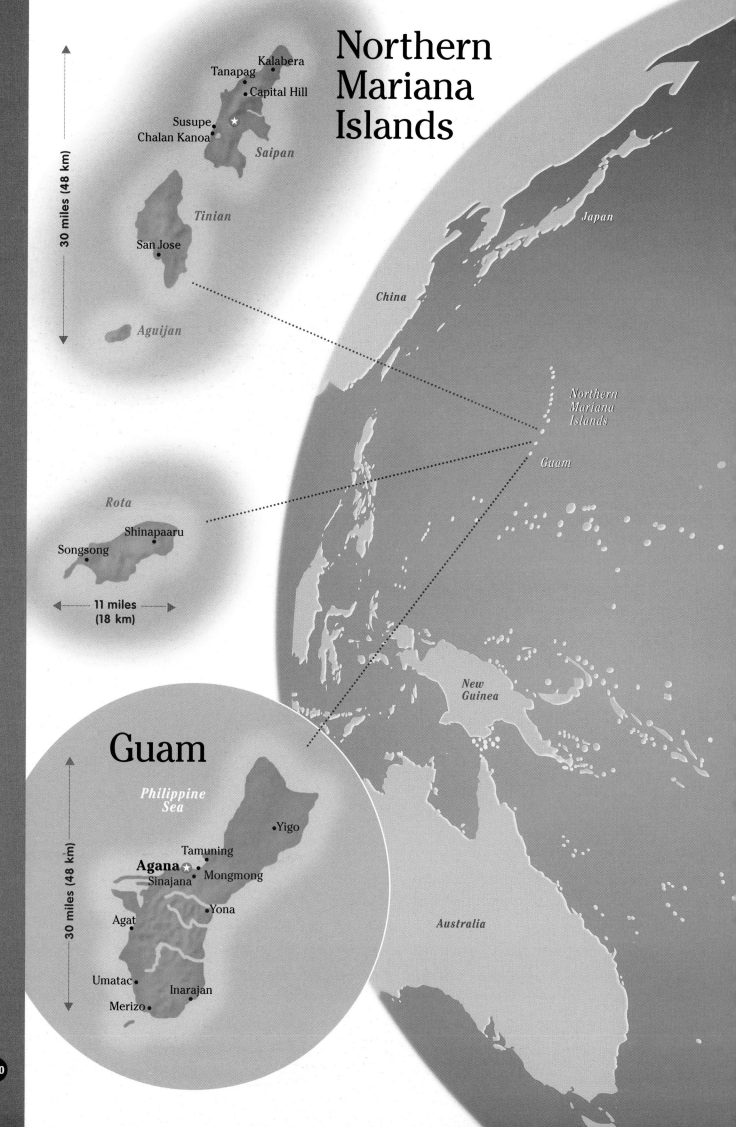

Northern Mariana Islands

Kalabera
Tanapag
Capital Hill
Susupe
Chalan Kanoa
Saipan

Tinian

San Jose

Aguijan

30 miles (48 km)

Rota

Shinapaaru
Songsong

11 miles
(18 km)

Japan

China

*Northern
Mariana
Islands*

Guam

*New
Guinea*

Australia

Guam

*Philippine
Sea*

Yigo
Tamuning
Agana
Mongmong
Sinajana
Yona
Agat
Umatac
Inarajan
Merizo

30 miles (48 km)

Pacific Possessions

Aleutian Islands

PACIFIC OCEAN

Hawaii

American Samoa

National Park of American Samoa

Tutuila

• Tula

Pago Pago • Fagatogo

Aunuu

• Nuuuli

Leone •

• Iliili

20 miles
(32 km)

Olosega

Ofu

Tau

Tau • • Maia

Manua Islands

National Park of American Samoa

18 miles
(29 km)

American Samoa

Western Samoa

Fiji

Tonga

U.S. Population Density

CANADA

PACIFIC OCEAN

MEXICO

GULF OF MEXICO

ATLANTIC OCEAN

POPULATION DENSITY
(people per square mile)

- fewer than 2
- 2 to 24
- 25 to 125
- more than 125

Major U.S. River Systems

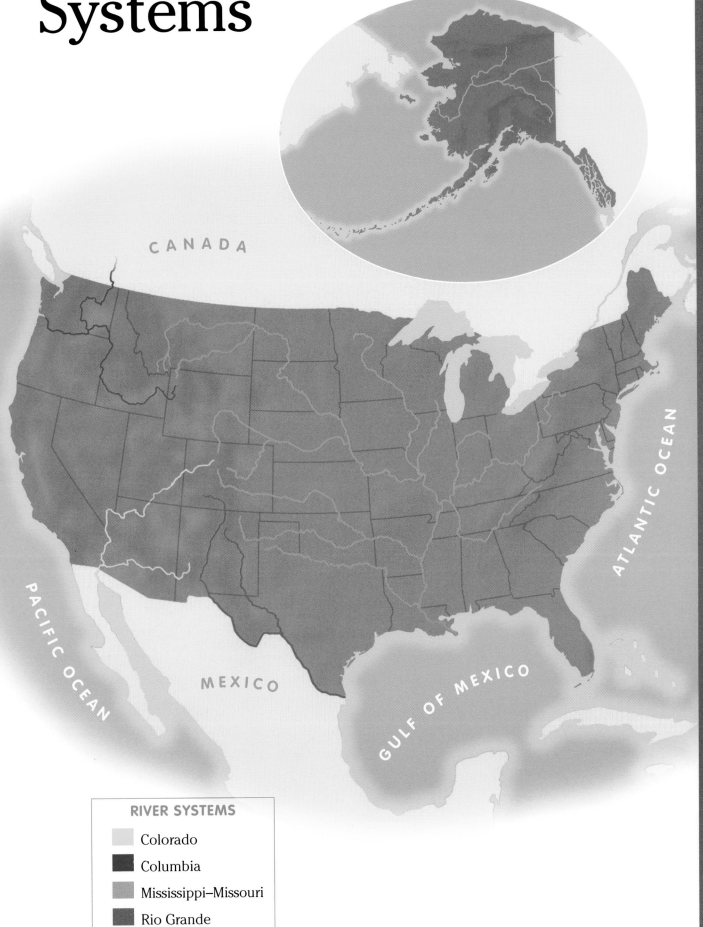

CANADA

PACIFIC OCEAN

MEXICO

GULF OF MEXICO

ATLANTIC OCEAN

RIVER SYSTEMS
- Colorado
- Columbia
- Mississippi–Missouri
- Rio Grande
- Yukon

U.S. Geographic Regions

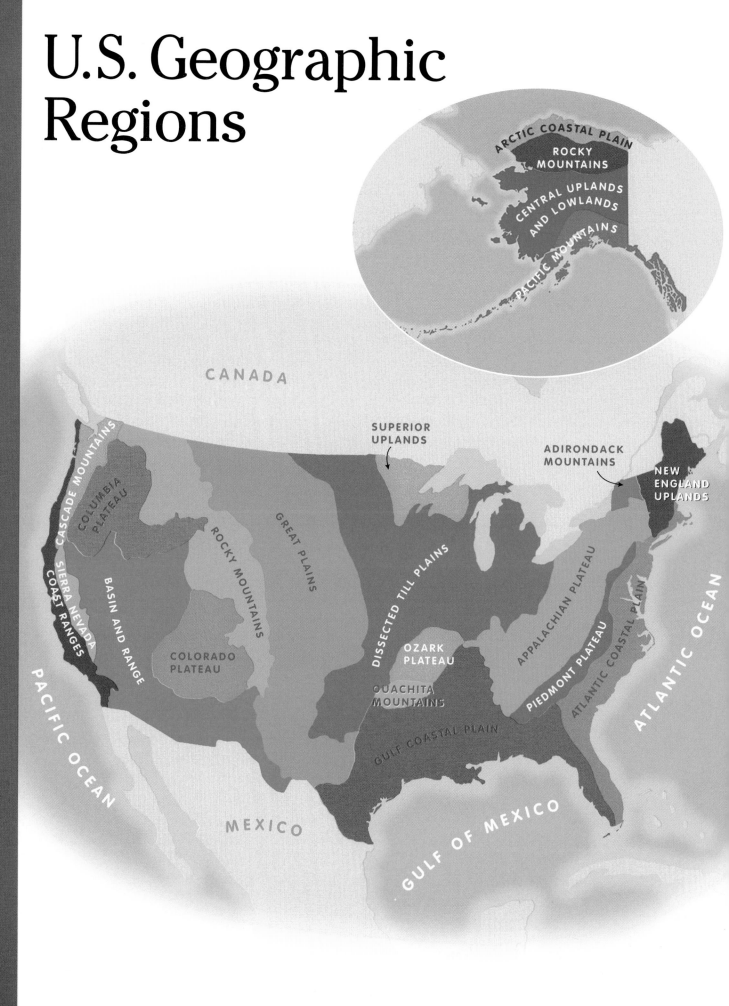

ARCTIC COASTAL PLAIN
ROCKY MOUNTAINS
CENTRAL UPLANDS AND LOWLANDS
PACIFIC MOUNTAINS

CANADA

SUPERIOR UPLANDS

ADIRONDACK MOUNTAINS

NEW ENGLAND UPLANDS

CASCADE MOUNTAINS

COLUMBIA PLATEAU

ROCKY MOUNTAINS

GREAT PLAINS

SIERRA NEVADA

COAST RANGES

BASIN AND RANGE

COLORADO PLATEAU

DISSECTED TILL PLAINS

OZARK PLATEAU

OUACHITA MOUNTAINS

APPALACHIAN PLATEAU

PIEDMONT PLATEAU

ATLANTIC COASTAL PLAIN

ATLANTIC OCEAN

GULF COASTAL PLAIN

PACIFIC OCEAN

MEXICO

GULF OF MEXICO

U.S. Territorial Expansion

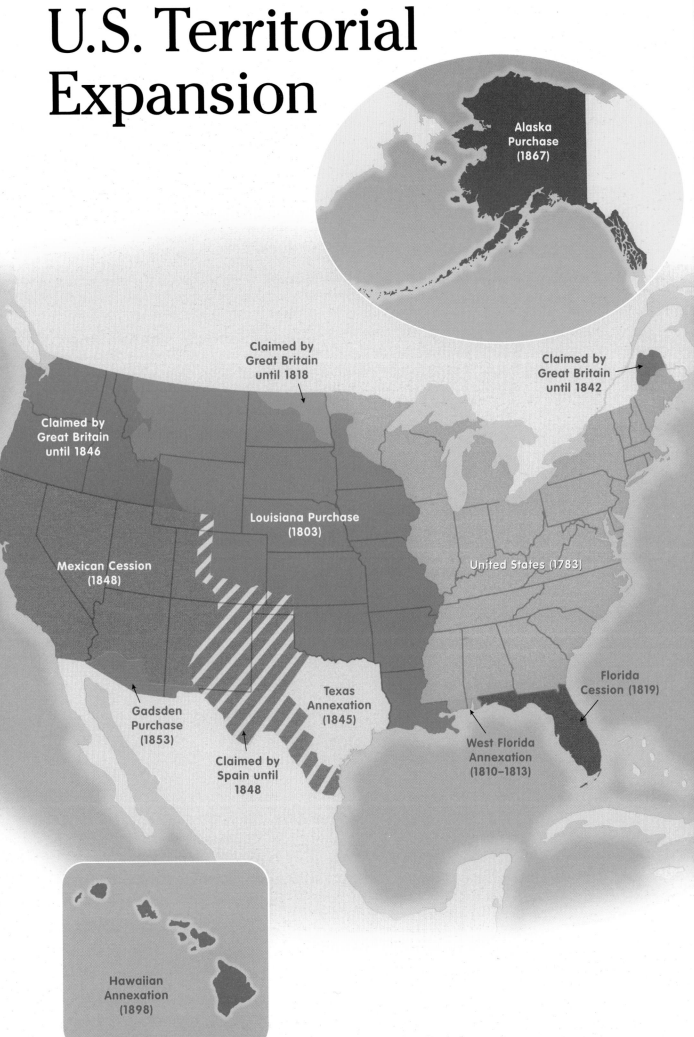

Alaska Purchase (1867)

Claimed by Great Britain until 1818

Claimed by Great Britain until 1842

Claimed by Great Britain until 1846

Louisiana Purchase (1803)

Mexican Cession (1848)

United States (1783)

Gadsden Purchase (1853)

Texas Annexation (1845)

Claimed by Spain until 1848

West Florida Annexation (1810–1813)

Florida Cession (1819)

Hawaiian Annexation (1898)

Glossary

aquifer   an underground layer of rock, sand, or gravel that holds water

arable   suitable for growing crops

arid   excessively dry; also, receiving too little rainfall to support agriculture

atoll   a coral island consisting of a reef encircling a lagoon

bald   a treeless hilltop

basin   a depression in the earth's surface; also, the area drained by a river and its tributaries

bayou   a slow-moving creek

bedrock   solid rock underlying a surface layer of soil

bluff   a high steep bank or cliff

bog   an area of wet, spongy ground

bottomland   a low-lying region along a waterway

butte   an isolated hill or mountain with steep sides (smaller than a mesa)

canal   an artificial waterway constructed to aid navigation

canyon   a deep narrow valley with steep sides, often with a stream or river flowing through it

channel   a narrow passage of sea between two close landmasses

Continental Divide   the principal watershed of North America, separating the Atlantic and Pacific ocean basins

continental United States   the coterminous landmass of the United States, composed of forty-eight states (excluding Alaska and Hawaii)

crater   the bowl-shaped depression atop a volcano

delta   the land created by sediment deposits at the mouth of a river

divide   a watershed, or dividing ridge between drainage areas

drift   debris transported by a glacier

escarpment   a cliff or steep slope between two level surfaces

estuary   the area in which an ocean tide meets a river current

fall line   the line along which a plateau drops abruptly, creating river rapids and waterfalls

fault   a fracture in the earth's crust

floodplain   level land occasionally submerged by floodwaters

foothills hilly region at the base of a mountain range

front the line defining the base of a mountain range

glaciation the process, or result, of being covered by a glacier

glacier a huge sheet of ice

gorge a narrow canyon

head of navigation the point on a river past which ships cannot travel

kettle lake a steep-sided lake formed by a glacier

levee a raised structure built to keep a river within its channel (and thereby prevent flooding)

loess soil composed of dirt deposited by the wind

mesa an isolated, flat-topped elevation of land (smaller than a plateau)

monadnock an isolated plug of granite that becomes a mountain after the surrounding land erodes away

oxbow lake a curved lake formed when a meandering river takes a more direct course, isolating a bend

peninsula a spit of land bounded on three sides by water

plateau a large, generally flat area rising above the surrounding land on at least one side

prairie mostly level or rolling land characterized by deep fertile soil, plentiful grass, and few trees

precipitation water deposited by clouds in the form of hail, mist, rain, sleet, or snow

rangeland land suitable for grazing livestock

sediment material deposited by water, wind, or glaciers

silt sediment deposited by moving water

subsoil the layer of weathered material underneath the topsoil

tableland broad, level, elevated land, as a plateau

terminal moraine rocky debris deposited at the front edge of a glacier

tidal river a river whose current is periodically affected (or reversed) by the force of ocean tides

tidewater low-lying coastal land characterized by numerous tidal rivers

till glacial drift containing a mixture of clay, sand, gravel, and boulders

topography the physical features of a region of land

topsoil the organic layer of soil closest to the surface into which plants sink their roots

tributary a river or stream that flows into a larger watercourse

tundra a level or rolling treeless plain with a permanently frozen subsoil

watershed a region, bounded by divides, draining into a particular body of water

Index

Index

Photo Credits

Greater Hartford Tourism District/Paul Conee: 10; Robert Perron: 11(l); Mohegan Sun: 11(r); Northern Maine Development Commission: 12; Acadia National Park: 13(l); Kindra Clineff: 13(r), 14, 15(l); Genetics Institute/Susan Lapides: 15(r); Tom Pantages: 16; New Hampshire Office of Travel and Tourism Development: 17(l); Rhode Island Tourism Division: 18, 19(l); Vermont Department of Tourism and Marketing: 20, 21(l); Delaware Tourism Office: 25(l); Winterthur Museum: 25(r); Baltimore Orioles/Jerry Wachter: 26; Maryland Film Office: 27(r); Port Authority of New York and New Jersey: 28; New Jersey Agricultural Society: 29(l); New Jersey Commerce & Economic Growth Commission/Scott Barrow: 23, 29(r); New York Stock Exchange: 30; New York State Department of Economic Development: 31(both); Hershey Community Archives: 32; Commonwealth Media Services: 33(l); Pennsylvania Game Commission: 33(r); Julia Rubel: 34; Alabama Bureau of Tourism & Travel: 38, 39(r); Alabama Farmers Federation: 37, 39(l); National Chicken Council/Richard Lobb: 40; Arkansas Department of Parks & Tourism/A. C. Haralson: 41(both); Everglades National Park 43(l); Greater Miami Convention & Visitors Bureau/Carl Purcell: 43(r); Georgia Department of Industry, Trade & Tourism: 44; Carpet and Rug Institute: 45(r); Kentucky Department of Surface Mining: 46; Kentucky Department of Travel: 47(both); Louisiana Office of Tourism: 49(r); Catfish Farmers of America: 50; Robert Perron: 51(l); Oxford Tourism Council/Ken Murphy: 51(r); North Carolina Division of Tourism, Film & Sports Development: 52; Dare County Tourist Bureau: 53(l); Cherokee Tribal Travel & Promotion Office: 53(r); CMI Industries: 54; Myrtle Beach Area Chamber of Commerce: 55(l); Oak Ridge National Laboratory: 56(both); Great Smoky Mountains National Park: 57(l); Tennessee Tourist Development: 57(r); Newport News Shipbuilding: 58; Virginia Tourism Corporation: 59(l); Colonial Williamsburg Foundation: 59(r); West Virginia Division of Tourism/Gerald S. Ratliff: 60; Monongahela National Forest: 61(l); West Virginia Public Radio: 61(r); Highway Images/Bette S. Garber: 64; City of Chicago/Peter J. Schulz: 65(l); Indiana Geological Survey: 67(l); Indiana High School Athletic Association/Mark Wick: 67(r); Jolly Time Pop Corn: 68; Iowa Division of Tourism/Bob Coyle: 69(l); University of Iowa/Tom Jorgensen: 69(r); Ford Motor Company: 70; Travel Michigan: 71(l); Wisconsin Department of Tourism: 71(r); Cliffs Mining Services: 72; Minnesota Office of Tourism: 73(l); Minnesota Public Radio/Fredric Petters: 73(r); Fire Master Fire Engines: 74; Missouri Division of Tourism: 75(l); Truman Library: 75(r); Akron/Summit Convention & Visitors Bureau: 76; Ohio Division of Travel and Tourism: 77(both); Miller Brewing: 78; Wisconsin Department of Tourism: 79(l); EAA/Ken Lechtenberg: 79(r); Raytheon: 82; Kansas Wheat Commission: 83(l); *Emporia Gazette:* 83(r); National Cattlemen's Beef Association: 84; Stock Boston/Michael Collier: 85(l); University of Nebraska Athletic Department/ Joe Mixan: 85(r); North Dakota Wheat Commission/ Norma Anderson: 86; OBS Specialty Vehicles: 87(r); Citibank (South Dakota), N.A.: 88; South Dakota Tourism: 89(both); North American Aerospace Defense Command: 92; Colorado Travel & Tourism Authority: 93(l); Keystone Mountain/Ben Blankenburg: 93(r); Clear Springs Foods: 94; Nez Perce National Forest: 95(l); Peregrine Fund/ Russell Thorstrom: 95(r); Brodin Landing Nets: 96; Glacier National Park: 97(l); Travel Montana/M. Gurnett: 97(r); Thiokol Corporation: 98; Utah Travel Council: 99(both); Petroleum Association of Wyoming: 100; Wyoming Division of Tourism: 101(l); Cheyenne Frontier Days: 101(r); ASARCO: 104; Metropolitan Tucson Convention & Visitors Bureau/Gill Kenny: 105(both); Las Vegas News Bureau: 106; Mark Farmer: 107(r); Los Alamos National Laboratory/ Leroy Sanchez: 108; Taos County Chamber of Commerce/Susan Christie: 109(l); Indian Pueblo Cultural Center: 109(r); Oklahoma Tourism/Fred W. Marvel: 110; Samuel Roberts Noble Foundation: 111(l); King Ranch, Kingsville, Texas: 112; Wildseed Farms: 113(l); Austin Convention & Visitors Bureau: 113(r); Alyeska Pipeline: 116; National Park Service/Bob Richey: 117(l); Anchorage Convention & Visitors Bureau: 117(r); California Division of Tourism/Robert Holmes: 119(l); Chez Panisse/Franklin Avery: 119(r); Hawaii Visitors & Convention Bureau: 120, 121(l); Lewis Rosman: 121(r); Oregon Tourism Commission: 122, 123(l); David Falconer: 123(r); Bureau of Reclamation: 124; Mount St. Helens National Volcanic Monument: 125(l); Bellingham/Whatcom County Convention & Visitors Bureau: 125(r); Corbis: 9, 17(r), 19(r), 21(r), 24, 27(l), 35(both), 42, 45(l), 48, 49(l), 55(r), 63, 65(r), 66, 81, 87(l), 91, 103, 107(l), 111(r), 115, 118.